Technology Integration
in the
21st Century Classroom

Anthony G. Brewer

with contributions from Chadd A. Brewer

Production
Ken Harvey

Copy Editor
Sharleen Nelson Bolkan

Cover Design
Tim Yost

Project Technology Consultant
Chadd A. Brewer

© **Visions Technology in Education, 2003**

P.O. Box 70479
Eugene, OR 97401
Phone: 541.349.0905   Order Desk: 800.877.0858
Fax: 541.349.0944   Order Fax: 800.816.0695
Email: info@visteched.net   Web site: www.toolsforteachers.com

ISBN: 1-58912-231-3

From the Publisher

Visions Technology in Education develops and publishes material for teachers, students, parents, and educational leaders. By producing field-tested resources to assist in the teaching/learning process, Visions aims to utilize technology to better serve students and educators alike.

Our wide variety of books and software promotes interactive learning on a personal basis as well as in a classroom or training context. With the increasing expectations placed upon educators to meet the needs of special learning groups, as well as striving to stay current with rapidly changing technology, we seek to select quality materials that assist you in both endeavors.

We desire to provide affordable resources to "help you help others." Please let us know how we can be more effective by sharing your ideas and opinions with us.

Acknowledgments

I would like to thank the following people and organizations for their kind help in the development of this book:

Ms. Karen Fuller for her support and dedication in editing this Architext Inc. book, as well as for her many excellent suggestions; Mr. Chadd Brewer for his excellent consulting services for the System Administrator technology side of the book; educators from around the world for their suggestions; and finally, classroom teachers for their K–12 ideas during and after attending my countless technology presentations and workshops.

"Imagination is more important than knowledge."

— Albert Einstein

Table of Contents

Section 4: Educational Mailing Lists

Section 5: Educational Newsgroups

Section 6: The World Wide Web

Section 7: Citing Online Resources

Section 8: Evaluating Web Sites

Section 9: A Good Back-Up Plan

Section 10: Internet Lesson Plans

Section 11: Internet Classroom Projects

Section 12: WebQuests in the Classroom

Section 13: The One-Computer Classroom

Section 14: Copyright, Plagiarism & the Internet

Section 15: Student Assessment & Electronic Portfolios

Section 16: Summation

Index

Introduction

Our most important resource is other human beings. If you do not know the answer to a question, chances are that someone else does and, there are "ask an expert" programs all over the Internet ready to help answer those questions. Later in the book I will tell you how to contact them. The fastest method of communicating with them or anyone else is via email. Email allows us to communicate with someone in Europe in mere seconds—let's see the Post Office do that! Because I travel more than 100,000 miles a year instructing teachers in how to integrate technology into their classrooms, I have little or no time to use the phone, not to mention the sums of money it takes for long distance phone calls. Therefore, I rely on email as my main method of communication.

I receive as many as 300 email messages a week. If I had to answer each request for information or help using the U.S. Postal Service, I would be spending nearly $160 per week on postage. However, with my Internet account, I only pay a monthly service charge of $17.95. With that account, I have complete access to the vast wealth of information available on the Internet, such as audio clips, video, photographs, and text. I can take virtual tours of the White House, view the Louvre in Paris, and the Grand Canyon. I can visit communities, make airline reservations, send flowers to my mother in Mobile, download tax forms from the IRS (a somewhat scary thing to do the first time), and even review the bills currently before Congress. I can visit NASA, see the Hope diamond, and learn about the Sioux Nation at their home page. With the click of my mouse, I am able to turn my computer into a jet plane, flying from city to city around the world without ever leaving the comfort of my easy chair.

Some other examples of the usefulness of the Internet include the ability to check your stock investments online, take virtual test drives of your dream car, and even purchase groceries over the Internet. Ordering tickets for your favorite sporting event, making dinner reservations for that special anniversary, or booking the hotel for that weekend getaway is only a mouse click away.

In addition, the Internet is chock full of mailing lists, Usenet newsgroups, and other discussion groups for you to join. There are more than 17,000 Newsgroups in existence on the Internet. From Astronomy to Zoology, Newsgroups offer something for everyone. Having trouble rebuilding that '56 Chevy engine, or wondering whether municipal bonds are a good purchase right now? Find the answers to these and a million other questions on the Internet.

The Internet benefits students even more. With a click, they can gather information about their science projects, get help with their homework, and communicate with experts around the world. They can join global scientific expeditions such as *Blue Ice* or *MayaQuest*, or discover ways to create their own Internet projects or "WebQuests" through collaboration with global peers.

Every day, new technology is emerging that allows faster, clearer, and more cost-effective ways to communicate. Good luck on your journey.

How Will this Book Help You, As an Educator?

It was my intention to make this book both easy to read and user friendly. To achieve that goal, I have removed much of the needless "technobabble" without leaving the reader feeling alone in cyberspace without a star chart.

In addition, I have taken a different approach to teaching technology integration in this book by organizing it in a way that addresses the main issues, or things you need to know quickly to understand how the Internet and all its information-gathering tools work. It is a step-by-step, fast reading version of all the technical information that others have tried to get you to understand.

Each page is linked to the next in a way that allows you to go back just one page if you get lost along the way. I have included screen captures of what you will see on your monitor for each topic discussed.

I have successfully trained thousands and thousands of teachers around the world using this method. I know your adventure will be equally successful.

As a parent or teacher, the issue of inappropriate material probably rates high on your list of reasons to not join in on the 'Net fun, so I've included information about software designed to help alleviate your fears, as well as provide some ideas on monitoring kids' online time.

The Internet does not care what kind of computer you have, and neither do I. Each topic looks basically the same in both Windows and Macintosh formats. Eventually, there will be one standard computer language used throughout the universe, making much more sense than all the chaos out there now. Bill Gates has already taken the first step by investing in Apple™. Whenever necessary, however, I have captured screens from both Mac and Windows to show you how to do such things as copying and pasting text and graphics from the Internet into a word processing document.

All you need to accomplish 99% of what you want to do on the Internet is a good Web browser like Netscape or Internet Explorer. I'll talk more about them a little later.

In this book, you will learn how the Internet got started, and the basic tools you will need to successfully navigate it. I have included World Wide Web sites for you to begin mining the Internet immediately. You will learn how to locate the Internet's search tools including Fossick, Google, Mamma, Vivisimo, and a host of others. You will also learn how to create a *keyword* search for the information you are seeking.

Teachers will learn how to create fun, exciting, multimedia-type lesson plans, as well as how to locate hundreds of thousands of them already online. You will learn what an Internet-based learning experience is all about, and how to locate, join, or create an exciting learning adventure for your class, such as a virtual tour of the Smithsonian Institute as shown below.

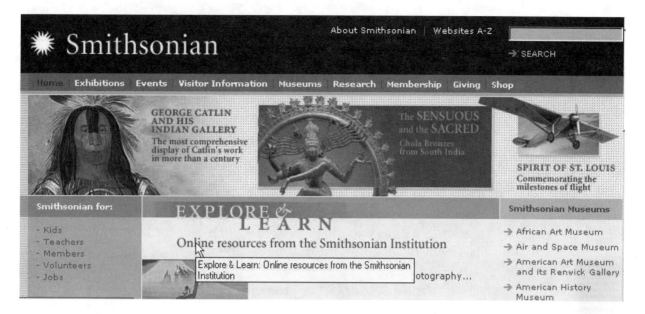

Technology is changing the way we teach, the way students learn, and the way the world thinks. As educators, we must continue to be flexible in our approach to teaching to help students become the knowledge workers of the 21st century. As Einstein said, "Imagination is more important than knowledge." We owe it to our students and to ourselves to find new ways to motivate and engage them in this new educational technology.

I guarantee if you can find something a student enjoys on the Internet, you will ignite a desire to participate in learning within that student like you have never seen before.

In addition, this book provides a look into the future to see what lies ahead for technology. You will discover just how close to reality the hit movie *The Net* really was.

Need to find directions to your mother's new house? We will visit MapQuest and show you something that will quite possibly blow your mind. Every house address in existence in the United States can be found online, along with its latitude and longitude noted. Students love this site and find many ways to integrate it into their online research assignments.

Making every effort to keep this book user friendly I have captured actual slides from my computer screen. They are placed in step-by-step order to avoid confusion. As long as your screen looks like the one pictured, you should have no difficulty following the logical procession of steps. In the event that the computer makes a mistake, simply go back one slide and start the process over. You will make a few errors along the way, but don't worry, it's the learning process that counts.

I have included many captures of Internet Explorer because there are few differences in appearance between it and Netscape. Choose whichever one strikes your fancy. The browser of your choice will look virtually the same on a Mac or Windows machine. Folks are always asking which I prefer, Mac or Windows. My answer is that I like elements of both platforms. While many support the idea that Macs are more user friendly, others contend that Windows is the "real" format. It's up to you to decide which best fits your needs.

What Equipment Will You Need?

As mentioned earlier, the Internet does not care what type of computer you own. The first requirement is that you feel comfortable with the machine you have and possess a basic understanding of how to turn it on, open files, use windows and programs, and how to shut it down. The following is a guide to the minimum requirements needed to operate on the Internet, along with my recommendations.

Ram memory: The program-operating portion of your computer. It allows you to run such programs as Word Perfect, ClarisWorks, Netscape, etc.

Minimum requirements:	128 megabytes
Recommended:	1 gigabyte or more

Processor: The chip that controls how fast your computer operates. The faster the processor, the faster you are able to perform various tasks.

Minimum requirements:	approx. 500 megahertz
Recommended:	approx. 1 gigahertz or faster

Hard drive: The real memory in your computer. This is where the vast quantities of text, graphics, video, audio, software, and anything else you might download from the Internet, CDs, or Floppy disks is stored. Please keep in mind that additional hard drive space is relatively inexpensive, and like money, you can never have too much. Text takes up very little hard drive space, whereas graphics, video, and audio consume sizable quantities. For instance, if you have a pick-up truck moving quickly along a 10-lane highway, that truck represents text being sent along a phone line to your computer's hard drive. It is done quickly and takes up very little room.

Now, picture 250 tractor-trailers clogging up the 10 lanes, all trying to stay together similar to a convoy. Those tractor-trailer trucks represent a graphic image being sent along the same phone line to your computer. It takes longer for the big trucks to load onto your hard drive because they take up a whole lot more space than a pick-up.

The answer is to get as large a hard drive as you can afford. Because the Internet is changing complexion everyday and moving more and more into graphics, audio, and video, you'll need a lot of hard drive space to accommodate the changes.

Minimum requirements:	20 gigabytes
Recommended:	50 gigabyte or more

Glossary of Frequently Used Terms

Before you begin your journey into Cyberspace, it is important for you to have a basic understanding of the technical terminology used in this book. While every effort has been made to provide a simple, user-friendly primer, there are a few new terms to add to your repertoire. Nothing is more frustrating than reading a book and having to refer to a dictionary every five minutes to look up a word.

Some of you may be suffering from *technofobic Paralysis*, a common aversion to the very thought of using computers. Fear not—I can assure you that while the Internet can, and possibly will, become addictive, you will not receive any unusual electrical shocks, brain wave overloads, or eyes that will begin to glow in the dark. (Unless, of course, you spill an RC cola on your keyboard.) What you can expect is to develop a good vision of the future—how we can communicate with one another, perform research at distant universities, track down lost relatives, or teach our students.

The Internet is, indeed, the most exciting, talked about topic at cocktail parties, K–12 schools, universities, and businesses across the country. Welcome aboard the Internet express.

Term	Definition
address	You or something that resides on the Internet, e.g., your email address.
Archie	A software program designed to search millions of computer files at ftp sites.
archives	Locations on the Internet where files containing information are stored.
baud	The rate at which data are transferred electronically using modems in bps.
bit	Currently, the smallest measurement of a unit of data.
bookmark	Placing a marker in a document, or saving the addresses of ftp, gopher, or World Wide Web sites visted on the Internet.
bps	Sometimes referred to as baud or the measurement of the speed of data transmission using a modem.
browser	A software program that allows users to surf the Internet to retrieve text documents, graphics, video, or other software programs.
compress	Condensing large files of information into smaller ones to save hard drive space.
Cyperspace	The sum total of the computers and networks interlinked through the Internet.
download	To retrieve a file from a remote computer via a phone line and modem.

email	Method of communicating with others electronically.
Eudora	A particular email program for both Mac and Windows users.
faq	Documents on information sites that list useful frequently asked questions about the subject being investigated.
Fetch	A particular ftp software program developed at Dartmouth University.
ftp	File Transfer protocol. The program used to upload and download files to and from the Internet, respectively.
gopher	Sites on the Internet that allow you to access files of information stored in menu form for ease of access. Currently, more than 6,000 gopher sites exist on the Internet.
home page	The opening screen at Web site.
html	Hypertext Markup Language. A coding program used to create Web pages.
hyperlink	A connection between your current location on the Internet and another Web site. Usually typed in blue, red, yellow, or green and as a colored line around an image on a Web page.
Internet	Networks of computers around the globe that are interconnected via phone lines, satellites, or cable TV.
Internet Explorer	A Microsoft software program that allows users to surf the Internet.
irc	Internet Relay Chat. A method of communicating with others over the Internet in what is referred to as "real time."
isp	Internet Service Provider. Generally, a commercial organization that provides access to the Internet via phone lines, satellites, or coaxial cable.
log off	To exit a particular computer.
log on	Signing on to a computer.
mailing list	Discussion groups communicating via email.
modem	The hardware used to send information from a computer in a language phone lines can understand, and then back into computer language at the receiving end of the transmission.
Mosaic	An early browser used to surf the Internet.
Netscape	A browser used to surf the Internet.
network	From a few to many computers connected to one another. The Internet is actually composed of networks of interconnected computers.
newsgroup	A place for like-minded people to meet and discuss a particular topic.
Pkunzip	Used to decompress files used by windows users.
ppp	Point-to-Point Protocol. A newer method of accessing the Internet using an Internet service provider.
server	A computer that acts as a host for others to use.
site	The location of a host computer somewhere on the Internet.

slip	Serial Line Internet Protocol. An older method of accessing the Internet using an Internet service provider.
telnet	A program that allows access to remote computers and uses the software on them as if it was a remote computer. With the advent of the Internet, however, telneting is going the way of the eight-track player.
Unstuffit	A software program that allows Mac users to decompress files.
url	Uniform Resource Locator. The method of identifying site addresses on the Internet.
username	The log on for accessing some remote computers. Also used when signing onto an email system.
Veronica	"very easy rodent oriented net-wide index to computerized archives." Actually, it's the software used to do keyword searches for information on gopher sites, much like Archie does with ftp sites.
wais	Wide Area Information Server. A means of searching many databases for specific information.

Certainly, there are many other technology related words you will encounter during your Internet travels, but these are the primary ones. Technology doesn't necessarily mean rocket science; it is actually more along the lines of popular science. The jargon comes with use and interaction with other Internet users.

Section 1 — Internet Basics

The History of the Internet

Most people aren't interested in the history of how something like the Internet got started, but I feel it helps to know the background of any new subject I'm about to learn—especially if the subject is as cool as the Internet.

The U.S. Military developed the Internet back in the mid-1960s. Actually, it was Military Intelligence. At that time it was referred to as the ARPANet (advanced research projects administration network). Many universities around the country were doing special research for the military and were allowed access to the ARPANet to make communicating with their Government counterparts easier. The ARPANet remained exclusively for the use of the military and these research centers for more than 20 years. In the mid-1980s, the number of computers on the ARPANet totaled about 1,000. By the end of 1989, however, that number had risen to well over 90,000.

The ARPANet ceased to exist in the early 1990s. The National Science Foundation, created in 1986, gave out grants to Educational Institutions for further research into the development of this network of computers, now called the Internet.

Since the early 90s, the Internet has grown rapidly. With the addition of gopher sites, and in 1993, the World Wide Web, the Internet's growth rate exceeds 10% per month.

The World Wide Web is doubling in size every four months or so and threatens to become the sole driving force behind the Internet. It has grown from a meager beginning of a few hundred sites in 1993 to more than nine million sites in four short years. The World Wide Web's point-and-click, CD ROM-like access to text, graphics, and software, along with its ease of mobility around the Internet, make it quite appealing to the masses.

Internet Review

The Internet consists of millions of computers located all over the globe, including more than 190 countries. Greater than 400 million people now have access and estimates show that more than 50 million kids in the U.S. have Internet access at home. Moreover, the total number of Internet users worldwide is expected to exceed 700 million people by the year 2010.

The Internet never closes; it's open 24 hours a day, 7 days a week, 365 days a year. As I was doing my income taxes, on April 15th of last year I realized I was missing a form. I flew into an immediate panic about being late and being thrown in jail. I quickly remembered my vast knowledge of the Internet and soon found my way to FedWorld's home page. From there, I navigated to the IRS home page where I located their Forms and Publications section, and easily downloaded the form I needed. I was able to finish my taxes and ended up playing golf that afternoon.

In the mid-1960s, the Government was sending and receiving data over phone lines at the "amazing" speed of 300 baud, which is like watching paint dry.

Today, we can send and receive data via a dial-up line in excess of 56,000 baud, which is nothing compared to cable to your TV set; would you believe its over 500,000 baud?

The Internet craze is everywhere; on TV, in Newspapers, even the Country and Western radio station I listen to has its own "Down Home" Web page and email address.

The Internet is becoming a part of our everyday lives with virtual shopping malls, easy access to remote libraries, lesson plans and educational projects, coloring books, and even a virtual frog dissection kit online. National Public Radio is online. We can read our favorite magazines and more than 2,500 classic books. If you can think of it, more often than not, you can find information about it on the Internet. The Internet is going to change the way we live—from sending letters to our mothers and buying products to paying our bills and transferring money in our bank accounts.

Section 2 — Technology in the Classroom

The Changing Face of Education

As educators, we are charged with the daunting task of trying to keep up with the ever-changing, often perplexing world of information technology, while continuing to teach our students the same information. In the recent past, we served as the *sage on the stage*, imparting all the wisdom of the universe to the kids in our classes. It was indeed a teacher-centered situation.

However, today's fast-paced, multimedia-driven classrooms are forcing us to move away from the old methods of delivering instruction. We must now become more of that *guide on the side* we hear so much about. We must, in essence, become "edutainers."

Organizations such as ISTE, (International Society for Technology in Education), as well as state departments of education are developing a whole new set of criteria for how educators will be evaluated using technology, what students are expected to know about technology, and how instruction is to be delivered.

Some of today's classrooms are filled with computers, projection devices, television monitors, whiteboards, printers, CD writers, and every other type of new technology available.

Unfortunately, that isn't the case in the vast majority of classrooms. Most teachers struggle with how to make use of a single computer in their classroom, while providing as much online time for their students as possible. The one-computer classroom is discussed later in the book.

So, what are teachers doing to span the digital divide, yet still deliver the content necessary for students to achieve success on standardized tests? The answers lie within the confines of this book. We address everything, from the foundations of technology integration (the 3 C's) to educational mailing lists, a study of the World Wide Web, a tutorial on proper search techniques, how to evaluate and cite online resources, creating technology inclusive lesson plans, developing a project-based learning experience, and, finally, developing a WebQuest.

We also take a look at some of the finest examples of teacher resources available online including: Teach-nology, EdHelper, EduHound, PBS, and many others.

Most teachers find the quantum shift to student-centered teaching with technology fun, exciting and, in many cases, revitalizing. Like anything in life, technology can only be what we want it to be. The choice is up to you.

Before You Begin Your Journey

It might be advisable to take a few minutes to complete a teacher self-assessment survey prior to beginning your journey into technology integration. It will also help you derive the most from this book. Many states, including California and Pennsylvania, have such self-assessment tools available on their state Department of Education Web sites. Be sure to check if your state has such a tool. If your state does not, you might consider using the self-assessment located at **Improvelearning.com**. Developed by my good friend Dr. Alex May, it covers all the necessary categories of technology, including integration. Schools across the country have found it invaluable.

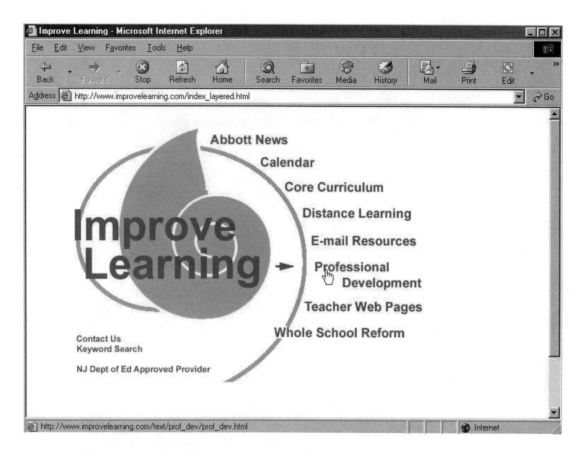

Click on **Professional Development**, and then select **Technology Self-Assessment**.

Fill in the requested information. If you are completing only your own self-assessment, then supply your email address to receive the report. If you are a technology director or principal, have your teachers' supply their respective email addresses so that the results come back to a central location. In this way, your technology directors or principals can quickly see which areas need to be supported by in-service training.

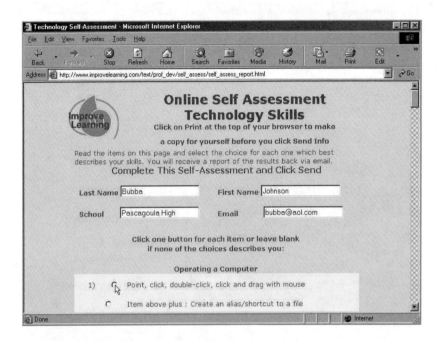

Click **Send Info**. Your report will come back shortly.

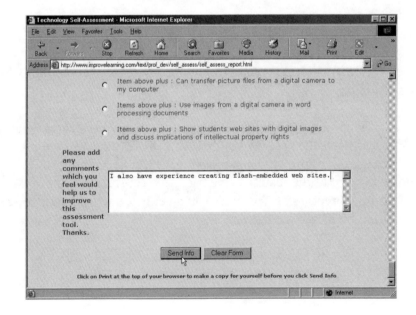

Section 3 — The Foundations of Technology Integration

The Three C's

Integrating technology into our classrooms is no longer a choice. The question most teachers face is not when, but how. As a result of the new national and state technology integration mandates, teachers everywhere are struggling to find ways to successfully integrate technology into their classrooms. I have spent the past 10 years circumnavigating the globe, trying to help teachers. After many years of research, trial and error, and input from educators like you, I finally arrived at certain conclusions. One, teachers, for the most part, want to learn to use the new technologies. Two, the fund of data covering what is expected and what tools to use is expansive and often confusing. And three, technology integration must be boiled down to it's lowest possible denominator for the process to occur.

The following foundations of technology integration, boiled down to the lowest possible denominator include **communication**, **computing** and **critical thinking**. By introducing one, two, or all of the three C's into your everyday lessons, you can successfully integrate technology into your classroom. The process is a lot easier than you might think, but keep in mind, less is often better than more.

Whether you have taught one year or three decades, integrating technology such the Internet into our classrooms is essential to properly prepare students to become the knowledge workers of the 21st century. The vast majority of jobs opening to students over the next few years do not yet exist. That is how fast technology is changing. By reducing the seemingly overwhelming technology integration task to the bedrock called the 3 C's, teachers more quickly and enthusiastically embrace it.

Communication

I strongly believe that people are our greatest resource. If I do not know the answer to a question or how to solve a particular problem, it's likely that someone else does. Knowing how to communicate with those who know the answers is almost as important as the answers themselves. In this day and age of "instant gratification takes too long," students want the answers now, not days or weeks later. Technology such as the Internet provides the perfect vehicle to accomplish this end.

Two basic types of communication can be used when integrating technology into our lessons. The first is communicating with another human being somewhere around the world. This may be a student's peer in a foreign country, across town, or an expert from NASA. The most common way to introduce students, especially in elementary schools, to online communication is by using KeyPals, or electronic PenPals. Kids love to communicate with one another and the use of KeyPals accomplishes more than one goal. Students not only improve their communication skills, but also their keyboarding, spelling, sentence structure, and in some cases, even their foreign language skills. Students are also learning to use technology such as email to perfect their copy and paste skills and to learn how to add attachments to messages. Excellent sources of KeyPals, or as some call them; Epals can be found at www.epals.com. It is a free service available in English, French, or Spanish for teachers and students. They have connected more than 900,000 students in over 12,000 classrooms from more than 100 countries.

The second type of communication using technology involves student communication with a remote computer. Again, the Internet is the vehicle. Students can be simply accessing a particular computer's database, if they know its URL (address), or searching for specific information on an unknown computer somewhere in cyberspace.

Along this vein, there are several main areas in which teachers need to be proficient to successfully integrate technology into their classrooms: good communication skills, proper searching techniques, copying and pasting from the Internet to a word processor, sorting and evaluating online resources, and citing online resources. After communication, using proper search techniques is the most important integration skill needed. Valuable classroom time can be wasted if students simply spin their wheels looking for information. The Internet is like your school library, only larger, with all the books thrown onto the floor and no card catalog. This is why proper searching techniques are so important.

An excellent searching tutorial using Boolean logic as a foundation can be found at http://home.sprintmail.com/~debflanagan/engines.html. Created by Deb Flannigan, this site teaches students how to conduct proper Boolean searching. Boolean searching is made up of "and or not" types of searches. For example, looking for information on Lions *and* Tigers, or possibly Cats, but *not* "broadway plays." When a student has located the correct information from the remote computer they need to copy it to their computer. This can be accomplished through downloading, copying and pasting, or by simply printing it out.

Computing

Now that students have learned how to search properly and locate the needed information, or have completed a research project where they have received data from participants around the world, they must do something with it. That can simply be printing it out, or saving it to a disk for later use. They may also immediately create a word processing document by copying and pasting. A word of caution here: information that has been copied and pasted must be used as a research tool only. Copying someone else's work is plagiarism. Be sure to have your students review the new MLA (Modern Language Association) or ALA (American Librarian Association) rules for citing online resources. You can find an easy tutorial on copying and pasting, as well as citing online resources at my Web site, http://www.tonybrewer.com/handouts.html.

The good old days of read a book write a report is rapidly becoming archaic. Instead, today's students are creating exciting and powerful PowerPoint and HyperStudio presentations to share with their classmates. They are now including pictures, charts, graphs, audio, and video files, as well as text. According to ISTE research indicates that when students are allowed to work as a member of a team to create a project or product they can share with their peers, community, and family, the greatest amount of learning and retention occurs.

Having students create their own charts, graphs, and computer-generated presentations often go beyond the original intent of your lesson plan, and that's a good thing. In addition to learning about the topic you have chosen, they learn how to communicate effectively, perfect their keyboarding skills, work as a team member, and enhance their public speaking abilities.

Today's teacher need not be the sole provider of knowledge and information in the classroom, because with the click of a mouse button an almost instantaneous wealth of information is now available to students. Technology such as the Internet is changing the way we teach, how students learn, and how the world communicates. It is up to us as educators to provide an open, supportive environment.

Critical Thinking

Most educators recognize the importance of students developing effective problem solving and critical thinking skills. The traditional instructional model of read, listen, and practice has worked well for learning lower level skills. While learning multiplication tables is certainly still an important part of developing a child's mind, today's students are faced with a whole new set of learning attributes, mainly technology. Today's teachers recognize that they must move to a more flexible type of instruction, in which students are more actively engaged in the process of their own learning.

Previously, I discussed communication and computing, two essentials in today's classrooms. Each has a very important role in helping students succeed with technology. However, these two attributes alone do not provide students with the skills necessary to achieve success in tomorrow's workplace. A student cannot succeed without the ability to sort good information from bad, or to view data without the ability to analyze it accurately. Using technology such as the Internet to locate information and spreadsheet, chart-, and graph-creating software to record that information is fine when we only wish to view that data for effect or comparison. To actually use that information for problem solving is another challenge altogether.

To help students begin using this new technology to it's fullest, and to promote critical thinking skills, I recommend that teachers introduce their students to new subject matter by using one of three basic types of project-based learning activities. The first is **Interpersonal Communication**, in which a student communicates via computer and modem with another student or expert somewhere in the world, or with another computer to locate information. The second is **Information Gathering** or **Data Collection**. In this model, students actually take the data from remote computers or other people and place it into charts, graphs or spreadsheets to view the data more effectively. The third type of project is **Collaborative Problem Solving**. This type of project requires students to place data into those same conveyances, and do a realistic scientific analysis of it. Each of these project types is addressed later in this book.

An excellent source of project ideas for your classroom can be found at Global Schoolhouses' Web site: http://www.gsn.org. Here, you will find hundreds of completed classroom projects, along with contact information should you wish to communicate with the projects' creator.

The success of computers in the classroom is directly related to a teacher's willingness to embrace new technology. I provide technology in-service training to thousands of teachers each year, and have witnessed the phenomenal growth of technology-assisted learning. However, having the technology alone is not the answer. It is the skill and knowledge of a teacher using a given tool or method that offers the greatest impact on student learning. Providing students with an effective, fun way to enhance critical thinking skills is essential to preparing them for the educational and vocational challenges of the future.

THE GLOBAL SCHOOLHOUSE

Welcome to the new home of the Global Schoolhouse!

Global SchoolNet is the leader in collaborative learning. We continue to provide online opportunities for teachers to collaborate, communicate, and celebrate shared learning experiences.

This website is free to all educators!

Section 4 — Educational Mailing Lists

What are Mailing Lists (Listserv's)?

Mailing lists, or Listserv's are nothing more than discussion groups using email as a method of communication. There are literally thousands of them to join, with subjects ranging from astronomy to scuba diving to automobile repair. They include discussions about movies, plays, books, and even pending legislation.

Moreover, hundreds of mailing lists are devoted solely to educators. Most of them contain postings from educators asking for or offering information about a particular educational question, where to find lesson plans, or inquiries about Internet projects for the classroom. You will also find a large number of requests for KeyPals, (electronic pen-pals). There are also lists specifically for library media specialists. And, because mailing lists are accessible all over the world, there's a tremendous amount of interactive multiculturalism.

You will probably need to spend some time going through the various lists to find the one(s) that fit your needs. Once you join a mailing list, you will receive postings to your email mailbox. Some of the mailing lists you join may yield 50–100 postings per day, so unless you have nothing else going on in your life, I recommend that you try a list out for a day or two and unsubscribe if the postings become too overwhelming. Eventually, you will find a perfect fit. I have listed a few of my favorite educational mailing lists later in this section. Try a few of them out and I'm sure you will find them invaluable.

Subscribing To a List

To subscribe to a list, you must send an email message asking to subscribe, or follow the easy directions offered by the list you wish to join. Below is the HILITES mailing list, one of the best and informative online for project-based learning.

To join HILITES, send email to
gsn-hilites-list-subscribe@topica.com.
You will receive an email confirmation
to validate your subscription.
**All you have to do is
REPLY TO that email message.**

You can
- Read more about HILITES,
- Browse recent archives
- Browse older archives from 1995-1999

Within a short period of time, you should receive a posting from the list, welcoming you and giving you instructions on how to unsubscribe if you ever decide to. Without the proper unsubscribe procedure, you could die of old age trying to get off a list. So, save yourself some aggravation and save that first posting somewhere or print out a hard copy.

Unsubscribe From a List

Follow the same instructions for subscribing to a list except type "unsubscribe" instead of "subscribe" in the body of the message. Because most mailing list moderators don't even look at the subject, leave the subject line blank. Some mailing lists require that you follow their exact method to unsubscribe to a list. That's why it is important to save the first posting.

Note: In the event you go on vacation or a sabbatical, be sure to unsubscribe from your selected mailing lists before you leave. Used properly, mailing lists can prove to be an invaluable asset, providing you with a wealth of information, lesson plans, and Internet project ideas and participants. Creating Internet lesson plans and projects is discussed later in the book.

Accessing and Using Mailing Lists

Literally thousands of online mailing lists address every issue known to humankind—from apples to zebras. Use mailing lists to receive information and discuss topics of mutual interest with others on the list. You may also meet some other great teachers out there.

Find a list or two you think you would like and subscribe to them in the manner described on the previous pages. Be careful not to subscribe to too many right away because some will send you postings several times a day or week.

Mailing list postings will come to your email mailbox just like messages from your friends and relatives. Read them at your leisure, reply to them, forward them to colleagues, save them to a file, print them out or delete them just like you would regular messages.

How Much Does it Cost to Join?

While I am sure that somewhere there is a mailing list that charges a fee to belong, I do not know of any. For the most part, they are free. I am quite sure you can find a mailing list in your area of interest without paying a fee to join.

There's a lot of noise being made about keeping the Internet pure and unspoiled by advertising. While we would all prefer this, it is a fact of life. Besides, I have seen some pretty interesting home pages that contain advertising. Advertising is actually paying for the Internet's content. That is a good thing.

Recommended Educational Mailing Lists

There are many excellent educational related mailing lists available for your subscription. I have subscribed to many of them over the past few years, and have found some to be extremely valuable. On the following page is a list of a few of my favorites. If you are not satisfied with any of these, conduct a search on the Internet (see search tutorial in Section 5) to locate science mailing lists or any other curriculum area you desire.

Kidsphere

A great K–12 teachers mailing list that provides daily postings from more than 20,000 educators from around the world who are asking and answering a wide variety of educational questions. KeyPals and Internet project ideas galore.

email to: kidsphere@vms.cis.pitt.edu

type: subscribe kidsphere (your name)

LM Network

A tremendous resource and a "must join" for Library Media Specialists. An extremely informative mailing list.

email to: listserv@listserv.syr.edu

type: subscribe LM_NET (your name)

Classroom Connect

The premier educator's mailing list on the Internet. This is another "must join" list that is brimming with daily KeyPal and project listings and requests.

IECC (Intercultural Email Classroom Connections)

This mailing list is like a giant warehouse in cyberspace. It is full of daily postings containing KeyPals and Internet project ideas for all curriculum areas.

email to: iecc-projects-request@stolaf.edu

type: subscribe

Global SchoolNet

An excellent mailing list for all discipline area teachers. This list puts you in touch with teachers from all over the world who are interested in creating a global learning environment for their students.

email to: majordomo@gsn.org

type: subscribe HILITES

EDNet

Another excellent mailing list. Like the others listed above, this list contains postings designed to enhance your classroom use of technology to teach the same old information in a new and exciting manner.

email to: listproc@lists.umass.edu

type: subscribe ednet <your name>

The above list is merely a sampling of the rich variety of mailing lists available. Lists exist for every K–12 discipline area, with further breakdowns into sub-categories of sub-categories.

An excellent list of educational mailing lists and all the other "public" mailing lists can be found at the Web address below. This site not only catalogs the lists, but also further breaks them down into number of current subscribers. This is an important feature because the more subscribers there are, the more mailbox postings you are likely to receive. The lists are also searchable and cataloged alphabetically by host site or by host country.

http://www.lsoft.com/lists/listref.html

Section 5 — Educational Newsgroups

What Are Newsgroups?

Newsgroups are discussion groups or bulletin boards on the Internet. Unlike mailing lists they do not come to your email mailbox, rather, you must go to them. While there are many similarities between them, they operate differently. Newsgroups can be discussions on any topic imaginable. At last count there were more than 17,000 different newsgroups in existence.

Accessing Newsgroups

Accessing a Newsgroup is easy. If you are using a browser such as Netscape or Internet Explorer, type the Newsgroup address (e.g., news:k12.teacher.chat) into the **Location** or **Go to** box, and then press **enter** (Windows) or **return** (Macintosh). The Newsgroup appears on your screen.

As an educator, you're probably interested in educational Newsgroups. For this purpose there are Web sites that provide a list of hyperlinked addresses for easy access. One such a site can be found at: http://www.hsv.k12.al.us/School/Newsgroups.html

Sending a Message to a Newsgroup

After you access a particular Newsgroup using Netscape or Internet Explorer, a screen opens displaying "Netscape News" or "Internet Explorer News."

Once you have read the postings from the Newsgroup you've selected, you may send a posting of your own for others who view the list to read. Below is a great site from which to launch your search for educational newsgroups.

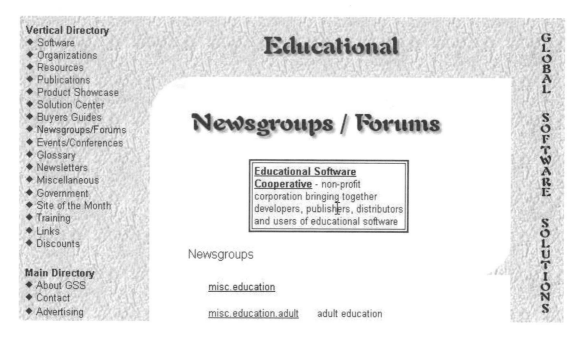

http://www.globalsoftwaresolutions.net/educational/newsgroups.htm

You will now see an email message ready for you to fill out, with the addressee being the Newsgroup for which you wish to communicate. Fill it out and click **Send**. That's all there is to it.

Starting Your Own Newsgroup

While creating your own Newsgroup is well within the realm of possibility, the uninitiated Internet user should not undertake it. One should log considerable time at the helm, reading and posting to Newsgroups that are perhaps similar to your proposed topic prior to trying to set up your own. To manage a Newsgroup requires spare time, something not many of us have. There are incoming postings to read, as well as posting of the messages themselves.

I discovered that it's much easier to simply join in on a few Newsgroups I enjoy. After all, with as many Newsgroups as there are out there, you're bound to find at least one that suits your needs.

If, however, you are bound and determined to do it yourself, you will need assistance. Probably the best place to begin your Newsgroup creation journey is at an existing newsgroup archive. The one I recommend is **Edunet**.

EDUCATIONAL NEWSGROUPS

Welcome to the Educational Newsgroup Resource listing. We are currently putting together a listing for Newsgroups that may be of use to educational establishments. This list is by no means exhaustive, but we will add more Newsgroups as we find them.

We would also welcome any contributions from you. Simply email admin@edunet.ie with a Newsgroup you would like to see here and we will add it for you.

Current Newsgroups:

There are no official or suggested rules of order for establishing Newsgroups. By emailing the above group of mentors, your Newsgroup establishment should go a lot smoother.

Section 6 — The World Wide Web

What Is the World Wide Web?

The World Wide Web is the fastest, most frequented part of the Internet. All over the world computers host Web sites, which contain a wide variety of interesting information, graphics, audio, and video clips. The information stored on these Web sites can range from a listing of lesson plans and virtual tours to a great collection of online WebQuests. With millions of Web sites already on the Internet, the number is doubling approximately every 6–12 months. The World Wide Web is, without a doubt, the number one reason use of the Internet is growing at such an astonishing rate. As speed of access increases, the number of Web sites visited per online hour will increase proportionately.

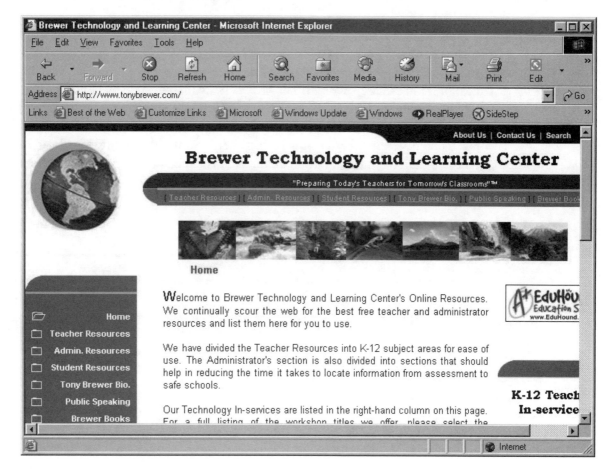

The World Wide Web is growing rapidly for several reasons, including its easy to use point-and-click method of access. Each Web site contains many hyperlinks, which may be a word or series of highlighted words, a graphic, or framing a photograph. Most of hyperlinks have colored text, so that they are easy to locate on a page filled with images, text, and sometimes advertisements. Any text in black type is typically not a hyperlink. The most common text color for a hyperlink is blue, but it's not unusual to find red, yellow and green hyperlinks as Web site creators search for new ways to draw attention to their sites. An easy way to determine if it is a hyperlink is to click the mouse on it. If it does not take you to another Web site or page within the current Web site, then it is not a hyperlink.

Another feature of some sites is the ability to place orders for products, register for a new version of software, or even download it directly from the Web site. This usually requires the use of your credit card number. While the chances of your card number being stolen is remote, it can happen. However, Some Internet Service Providers provide guarantees about the safety of your card number. If someone steals your credit card number and makes fraudulent purchases, they pay the charges. As the Web improves, cyberspace will become more secure. The latest versions of both Netscape and Internet Explorer provide SSL-v2 and SSL-v3 encryption capabilities, which can be set up in your Web Browser's **Preferences** folder prior to purchasing goods or services over the Internet.

Choosing a Web Browser

In this section, we access or "mine" the Internet using the Web browser Internet Explorer. There are several other browsers available, such as Netscape, or a relatively new one named Opera. You may choose the one you prefer, but I used Internet Explorer (I.E.) version 5.0 as my instructional browser of choice. There is not much difference between Web browsers. Some offer a few more bells and whistles than the others, but all in all, each is excellent in its own right. Below is a look at Opera:

I chose I.E. as my browser for many reasons. For one, it is extremely user friendly. The action buttons are highly visible and quick to use and it is organized in a logical manner. I.E. also features a **Links** bar that provides quick access to your most frequently used Web sites. The variety of search tools it provides is more than adequate, and easy-to-read buttons make navigation very easy. Additionally, I.E. includes its own tutorial handbook and announcements about new software. The Microsoft Outlook email program is easy to access and offers many useful extras. All you have to do is fill in the blanks. We take a closer look at Outlook later in this section.

Remember that Internet Explorer doesn't care what type of computer you have. The program appears the same whether you're using a Windows or Macintosh platform. Internet Explorer is an outstanding browser. The 5.0 version is especially user friendly. I recommend that you give it a try. You may find it better suited to your individual needs. Version 6.0 has been released, but I still prefer 5.0, at least for the time being.

Opening Your Browser

Below is a visual guide in how to open Internet Explorer, as well as the many features it provides. I have captured a slide or slides of each function to make following along on your computer easier. If you make a mistake, clicking on the **Back** button takes you back one screen.

First, let's look at opening I.E. Your ISP should include Netscape or Internet Explorer or both in your Internet access software package. If the one you want is not available from your ISP, you can download free one or the other from the Internet. Once you have a given version, you can then download subsequent new releases directly from the Netscape or Microsoft Web sites.

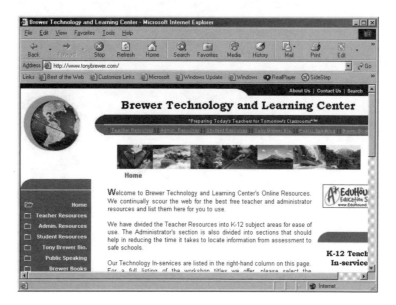

To use your browser, you will need to connect to the Internet via your ISP (Internet Service Provider), such as Earthlink or AOL. ISPs vary in their access software, so yours may look slightly different. Your browser can also be set up to automatically log-on to the Internet for you.

The following is a step-by-step tutorial for using Internet Explorer.

1. Log on to the Internet and access Internet Explorer by double-clicking your mouse on the appropriate icon. Or, you can set Internet Explorer to access the Internet as follows:

2. Select **Tools/Internet Options** from the top menu bar. From this screen, click the **Connections** tab and the following screen opens:

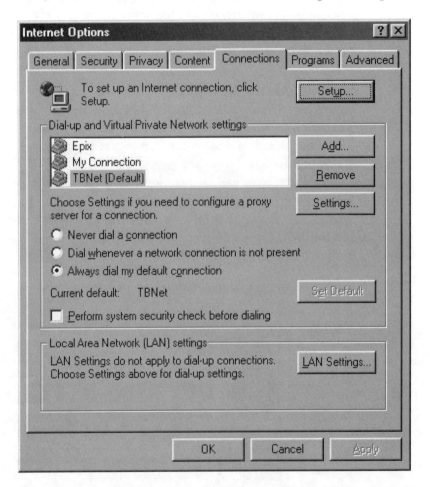

3. Click the **Setup** button to launch the Setup Wizard. At this dialog box, you may also add or remove ISPs from your list. You must select whether to dial a connection as shown above. This is also the screen used to access your Local Area Network (LAN) at school. You will need to receive the necessary information from your technology department to complete a LAN setup. In most cases, your school will only allow your tech department to make the necessary connections.

4. Once you have completed the previous steps, click the **Setup** button and the Wizard screen appears as shown on the next page.

5. Click on the button that best describes what you want to do; either sign up for a new Internet Account (you will need to do this when you first download and launch Internet Explorer), or to transfer your connection to I.E., or if you're accessing through your LAN.

There is also an excellent tutorial you may choose to follow. Click the **Tutorial** button and follow the easy step-by-step directions.

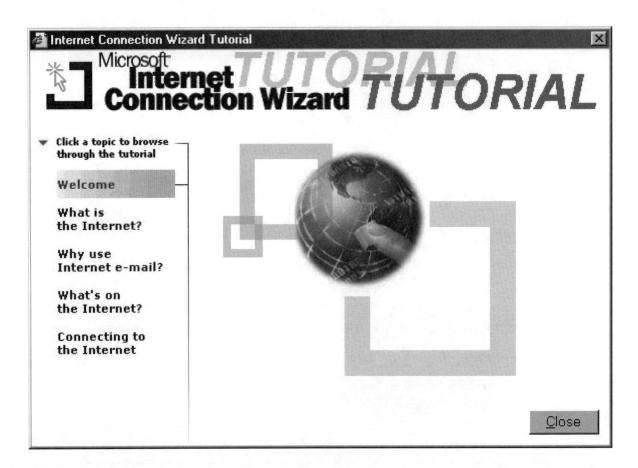

The tutorial helps you and your students learn about the origins of the Internet, how to use email, what's on the Internet, and how to connect to it.

Once you have set up your **Connection** preferences, Internet Explorer opens to whatever home page you designate in your preferences (see below). A home page is the first place you enter on the Web. Regardless of the site you choose, it will be the first page you see when you open your browser. If you create your own classroom Web site, you may wish to have it open as your home page.

Setting Browser Preferences

General Preferences tell your browser how to function. You can set Internet Explorer to start with a blank page or to a specific Web site. The following screen capture shows my preferences. You can select the same ones or modify it as you wish. Click-and-hold your mouse on the word "Tools" and scroll down to the words "Internet Options" and release your mouse. The **General Preferences** folder opens, as shown at right. Internet Explorer's preferences operate basically the same on both Mac and Windows computers.

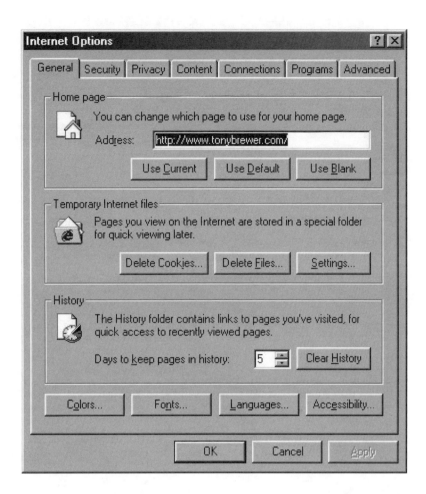

This screen also shows you where your Temporary Internet files are stored in the event you need to track where a particular student has been. Internet Explorer keeps a record of each Web site visited, as well as the time and date of each visit. To see where your students have been, click the **Settings** tab in the Temporary Internet Files portion of the screen. Then, select **View Files** on the next screen.

Note: It is important that students be notified in your school's **Acceptable Use Policy** (AUP) that emptying the Temporary Internet Files is justification for loss of Internet access privileges.

On the next page is a view of the **Temporary Files** folder. Notice that it also shows recent access to word processing documents. This folder also shows any cookies that have been placed on your computer. Cookies are picked up from visited Web sites that wish to gather information about your Internet surfing habits, or perhaps demographics regarding their particular site.

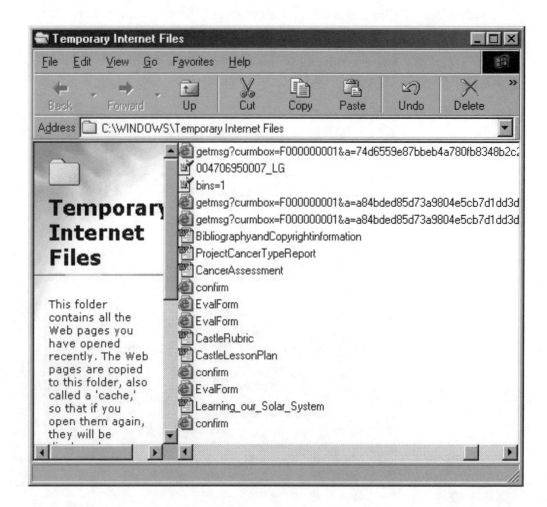

Be sure to check your Temporary Internet Files weekly, or more often if you believe a student may be abusing your school's AUP.

It may be necessary to periodically empty your Temporary Internet Files, because they can use up a lot of hard drive space. You may also choose to increase or decrease the amount of dedicated hard drive space by going back to **General Tab>Temporary Files>Settings** and using the sliding tab to reset the amount of space dedicated. To delete your Temporary Internet Files, or Cookies, go to: **General Tab>Temporary Internet Files>Delete Files**, or **Delete Cookies**. Be aware that some Web sites may not allow you full access to their site if you have deleted their cookie.

You may also decide how long Internet Explorer keeps track of your Web activities by returning to **General Tab>History** and selecting the number of days you wish to keep on file. To view the most recently visited Web sites, hold the small triangle down at the far right end of your **Address** bar. To clear this recent history bar, simply click on the **History>Clear History** button. (shown next page). This will *not* delete your Temporary Internet Files.

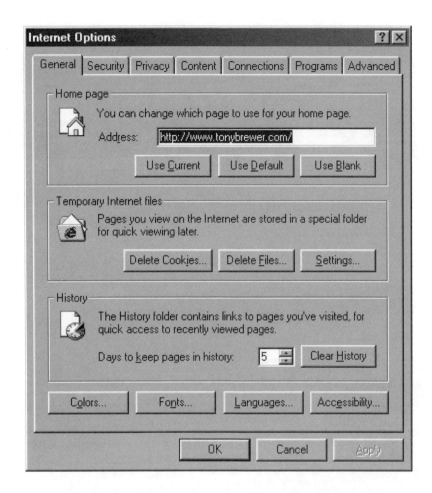

If you wish, you can continue clicking on the additional folders on the General Preferences page, such as Font, Colors, and Images and add your own preferences for each. It is fairly intuitive. If you run into difficulty, go to Internet Explorer's **Help** section for clarification.

Mail and News Preferences

Internet Explorer uses Outlook as its email program. You can set it up to be your email system as well. This may be advantageous in the event you are away from home or school without your computer and need to check your mail. You may use any computer that has Internet Explorer. The screen capture on the next page shows how to set up your email preferences. To access this screen, click-and-hold the **Tools** button while scrolling down to the words "Mail and News/Read Mail." The Outlook Wizard appears to help you through the setup procedure. It's an easy procedure and you will be sending and receiving email in no time.

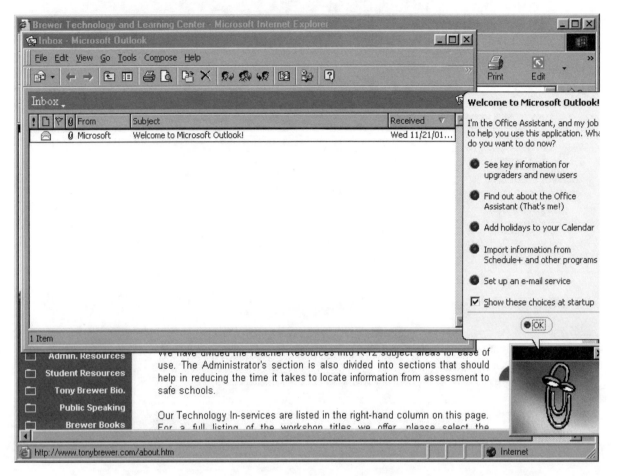

Microsoft is an intuitive program that you will learn to use very quickly. It's user friendly and interacts well with other Microsoft programs.

The screenshot below shows what the Outlook screen looks like when composing a message:

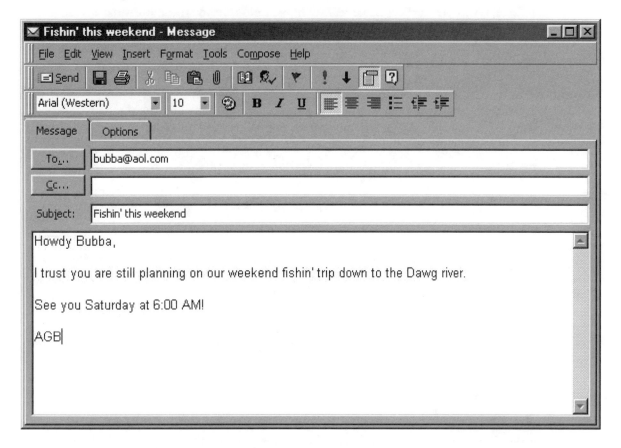

Notice that you can modify your message in many ways including font type, style, size, color, and much more. You may also choose to use a particular template for specific messages (see miniature below).

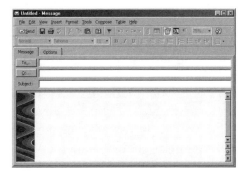

You may wish to continue setting your specific mail and news preferences, or to not use Outlook mail at all if your school provides you with a free email account.

Review of Internet Explorer's Other Features

Each button in Internet Explorer provides everything you need to explore the World Wide Web. The following is a glossary of these buttons:

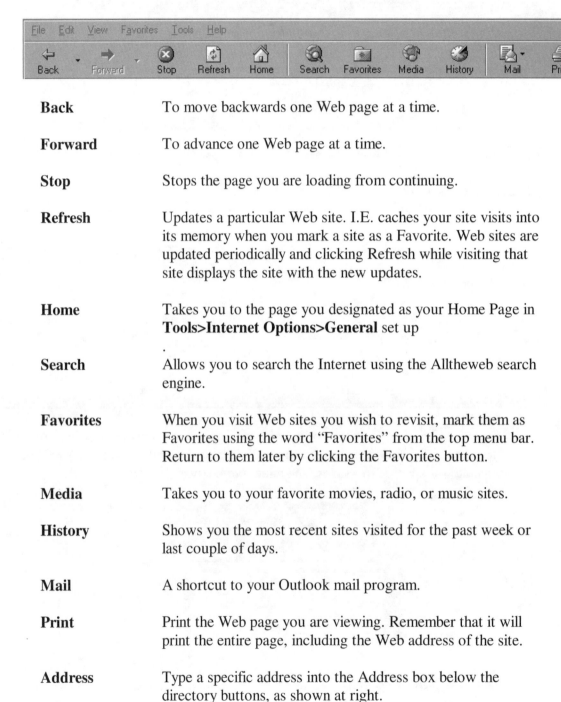

Back   To move backwards one Web page at a time.

Forward   To advance one Web page at a time.

Stop   Stops the page you are loading from continuing.

Refresh   Updates a particular Web site. I.E. caches your site visits into its memory when you mark a site as a Favorite. Web sites are updated periodically and clicking Refresh while visiting that site displays the site with the new updates.

Home   Takes you to the page you designated as your Home Page in **Tools>Internet Options>General** set up
.

Search   Allows you to search the Internet using the Alltheweb search engine.

Favorites   When you visit Web sites you wish to revisit, mark them as Favorites using the word "Favorites" from the top menu bar. Return to them later by clicking the Favorites button.

Media   Takes you to your favorite movies, radio, or music sites.

History   Shows you the most recent sites visited for the past week or last couple of days.

Mail   A shortcut to your Outlook mail program.

Print   Print the Web page you are viewing. Remember that it will print the entire page, including the Web address of the site.

Address   Type a specific address into the Address box below the directory buttons, as shown at right.

The main navigation buttons are intuitive. The **Edit** button is for editing your Web site using Microsoft FrontPage, a popular Web design program.

Another excellent feature of Internet Explorer is the **Links** bar beneath the **Address** box. This is where you place the sites you visit nearly everyday. These are shortcuts to them (see below).

To add a Web site to the Links bar:
Drag a Web page's icon from the **Address** bar to the **Links** bar, or drag any hyperlink from a Web page you are visiting from your **Favorites** bar or your desktop.

To remove a Web site from the Links bar:
On the **Links** bar, right-click on the Web site address you wish to remove, and then click *Delete*. For MAC, hold the mouse button down on the link you wish to remove and select *Delete*.

To rearrange the order of your Web sites from left to right on the Links bar:
Drag-and-drop any Web site on your **Links** bar to any location on the Links bar.

To customize Web sites on the Links bar:
Right-click the Web site address you wish to modify, and then click **Properties**. Then, click the **Change Icon** button to select a different icon for the shortcut.

Note: If the Links bar is not visible, from the top menu, click **View**, select **Toolbars**, and then click on **Links**.

To customize the look of your toolbar, select the two small greater than signs (>>) at the far right of the navigation buttons bar and select **Customize**. The screen capture on the next page shows most of the options.

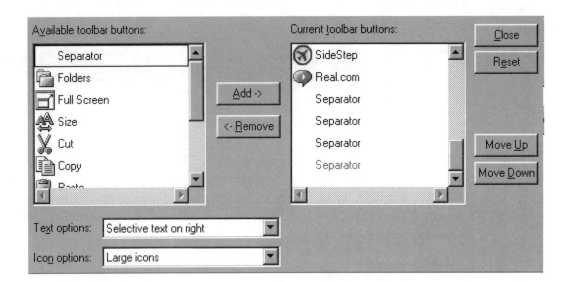

A Note about Plug-ins. A Plug-in is a small software program that enhances a browser's capabilities. If you wish to listen to select audio files, watch movies, download streaming video, view virtual reality sites, or talk to your mother over the computer, you will need some plug-ins such as Real Player or Media Player, QuickTime, Shockwave for Flash, and maybe a few others. Generally, when you visit a site that requires a plug-in, you will be notified if you need to download it. A good site to visit for plug-ins is: http://www.plugins.com/browser/

Exploring the World Wide Web

As an educator, you will be intrigued by the many wondrous learning opportunities the Internet affords your students. Section 10, of this book, deals with Project-Based Learning Experiences, where the real learning takes place. First, however, to gain a better understanding of how your browser works, I've included the following exercise:

Begin by opening your browser (see screen shot below). You may have set your browser's preferences to open to your personal page or another home page. Click inside the Address (location) box, (located between the Directory buttons and the Links bar), and highlight the address already in place. Type a URL (Uniform Resource Locator), the address of the Web site you wish to access.

In the example above, I have typed in the address for PBS, an excellent Web site that you and your students will thoroughly enjoy. It is an outstanding source of information on ancient Egypt, and contains a fun, virtual reality tour using QuickTime™ technology.

Note: Typing in URLs can be bothersome; it's easy to make a typing error. If you type in an address and receive a **No DNS Entry** dialog box, you've probably typed the address incorrectly. It is possible, however, that the Web site is no longer online. Browsers are defaulted to the ".com"domain, which means that all you need to type is the middle word(s) in the URL.

For example, if you wish to visit http://www.mapquest.com, simply type "mapquest." Your browser adds the rest of the address for you. Remember, this currently only works in the .com domain.

MapQuest is a free service for anyone wishing to use it. Use it to plan your next trip or print directions to your school for prospective parents.

After typing in MapQuest's URL, press the *enter* or *return* key, and the following Web site opens. Click on the hyperlink **Interactive Atlas** located in the center of the page.

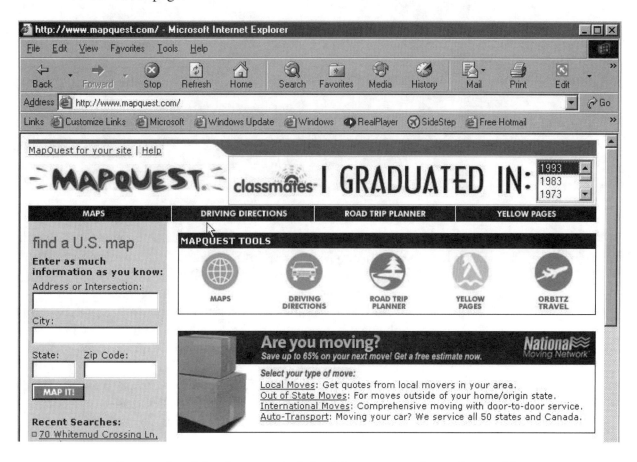

Locate the dialog box on the left of the screen and type in an address. When you are sure the address is correct, click the **Search** button. Be sure to provide as much information as possible; MapQuest is only as good as the data it receives.

The following map, or actually, one for the address you type in will appear, placing a red star at the approximate location you seek. Your students are sure to love this site. It will come in handy when you begin project-based learning experiences in your classroom, which require students to locate specific geographic locations. It is also handy for computing distance, creating scales to size, or plotting a summer vacation. Be sure to print out the maps as they appear and hang them around the borders of the room.

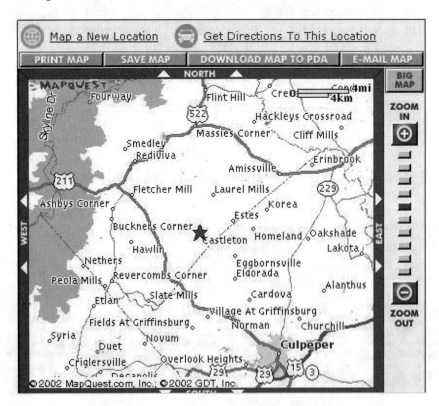

You may also zoom in or out, or pan left and right.

If you wish to map out a trip, let MapQuest do all the work. Click the **Back** button to return to MapQuest's home page. You may also go to the word "Go" on the menu bar and scroll down to MapQuests' home page. You will find this list invaluable for monitoring a student's online session.

Select **Road Trip Planner** and click the mouse on the hyperlinked button. The screen on the next page opens. Enter the city and state from which you wish to leave and the same for the place you wish to visit. You may also request "Door-to-Door" directions that include every turn in every road along your route.

Now, let's find the directions from Mobile, Alabama to Myrtle Beach, South Carolina. Type in a name for your road trip, click one-way or round-trip, and then enter where you are leaving from and where you are going.

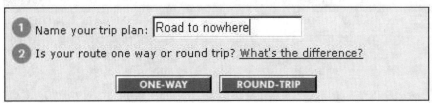

When you have entered all your information, click **Next**.

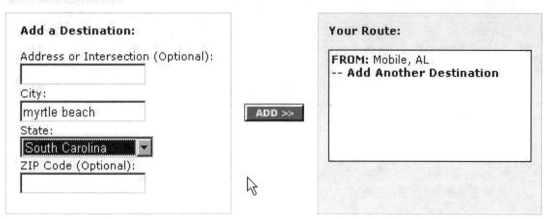

MOBILE, AL   MYRTLE BEACH, SC

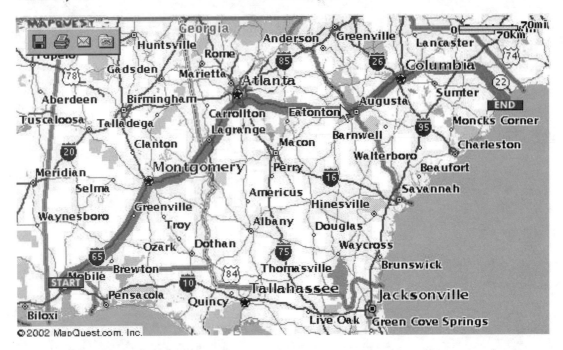

© 2002 MapQuest.com. Inc.

Road Trip Planner finds the fastest, most direct route. It returns a large map showing the starting point and the final destination. It also displays a close-up map of both locations. Scroll down farther to find the exact driving directions.

DIRECTIONS	DISTANCE
1: Start out going Northeast on DAUPHIN ST toward S WATER ST.	0.19 miles
2: Turn LEFT onto N WATER ST.	0.67 miles
3: Turn SLIGHT RIGHT onto US-43 N/AL-13 N/TELEGRAPH RD.	0.11 miles
4: Take I-165 N.	4.36 miles
5: Merge onto I-65 N via exit number 1B toward MONTGOMERY.	161.73 miles
6: Merge onto I-85 N via exit number 171 toward ATLANTA.	148.41 miles
7: Take the I-285-BYP E exit- exit number 68- toward MACON/AUGUSTA.	1.16 miles
8: Merge onto I-285 E/GA-407 E.	15.79 miles
9: Merge onto I-20 E via exit number 46B toward AUGUSTA.	276.33 miles
10: I-20 E becomes I-20 SPUR E.	1.79 miles
11: Turn LEFT onto US-76 E.	22.46 miles
12: US-76 E becomes SC-576 E.	3.11 miles
13: SC-576 E becomes US-501 BR S.	0.89 miles
14: US-501 BR S becomes US-501 S.	43.14 miles
15: Turn SLIGHT RIGHT onto 8TH AVE N.	0.03 miles
16: Turn RIGHT onto N KINGS HWY/US-17 BR.	0.33 miles
TOTAL ESTIMATED TIME: 11 hours, 38 minutes	**TOTAL DISTANCE:** 680.48 miles

Press the **Print** button at the top of the browser screen and you'll have a hard copy to take with you on the road.

If MapQuest has piqued your curiosity about the Internet, click on the location box, type in a new address and off you go. If you wish to return to the spot where you started, click the **Home** button. In the back of this book I have listed of some great educational World Wide Web sites covering every discipline area.

When you have completed your research, you may end your browser session by clicking-and-holding your mouse button down on the word "File" from the top Menu bar while you scroll down to **Quit**. Release the mouse button. You may also close your browser by clicking on the **X** box in the upper right-hand corner of Internet Explorer or Netscape.

Book-marking Your Favorites

As you explore the Internet you may wish to return to certain Web sites that you visit. To do this, you can **bookmark** sites into your **Favorites** folder.
Similar to using a bookmark to save a page in a book, you can mark Web sites to remind you of your place. You can organize or alphabetize your Bookmarks, save them to a file to attach to an email message, or delete them after they are no longer useful.

To establish your Bookmarks, launch your browser and type in a destination. If you're using Netscape, when you have the site on your screen, click on the word "Bookmarks" on the Menu bar at the top of the page. Scroll down to **Add Bookmark** and release the mouse. Your Book-marked site is now added to the bottom of your bookmarks list. You may also click-and-drag the address and drop it on top of the word "Bookmarks" to add it to your list.

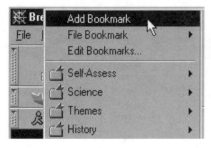 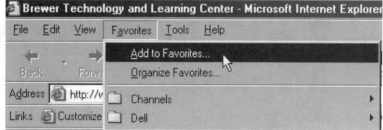

Netscape   Notice how similar the browser's look.   **Internet Explorer**

The process works the same with Internet Explorer, except Bookmarks are called **Favorites**. Grab the logo to the left of the address you are visiting and drop it onto the **Favorites** button at the top of your screen. With either browser, you may choose a particular folder in which to drop certain Bookmarks or Favorites.

Now that you have the idea of bookmarking, your instinct may be to bookmark every site you visit for a while. This, too, shall pass.

Because there are more than 100,000,000 Web pages for you to visit, you will probably never see a tenth of them. Bookmark only the ones you think you will use most often, for instance, **Search** tools such as Google, Vivisimo or Fossick. Bookmark your favorite lesson plans, WebQuests, and Internet project sites as well. Click-and-hold down the mouse button on **Bookmarks** while you scroll down to the bookmark of your choice. Release the mouse button and you return to your favorite site. You can organize your bookmarks into subject areas or in any order you desire.

Click and scroll down on the word **Bookmarks** or **Favorites** on your respective browser. Release the mouse and your Bookmarks appear on the left side of your screen with a colored ribbon or small icon in front of each. You can click and hold your mouse button down on any Bookmark or Favorite and drag it to any other position you wish.

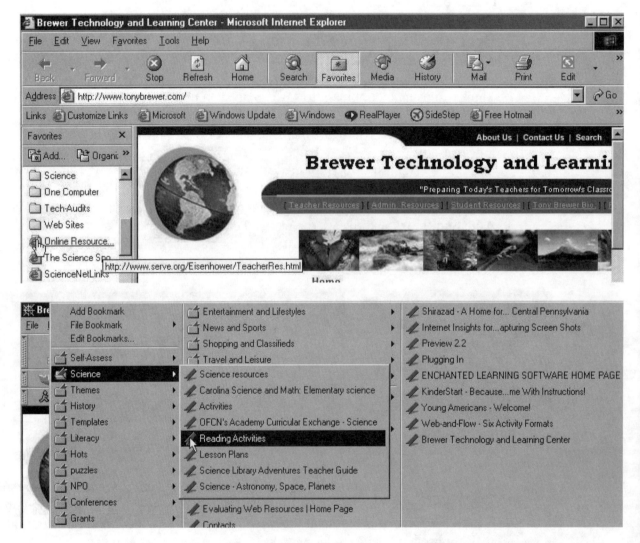

You may also delete any bookmark in Netscape by selecting **Edit/Delete Bookmark**. Once you have your bookmarks organized, click anywhere on your screen (off of your Bookmarks) and your bookmarks disappear.

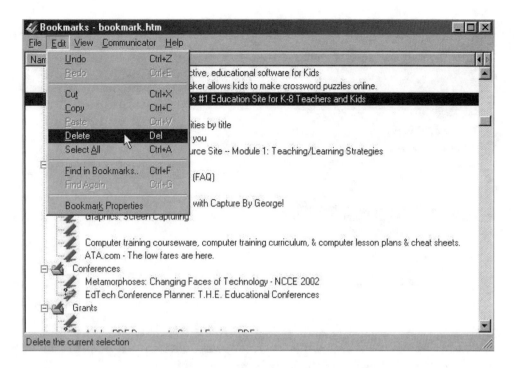

In Internet Explorer, select **Favorites>Organize**. Next, select the bookmarks you wish to delete and select *Delete*.

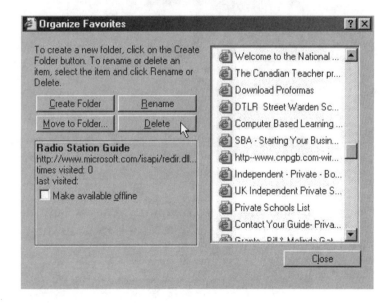

If you are concerned about your students accessing inappropriate material on the Internet, you can **Bookmark** certain sites that they may visit and no others.

Reminder: Because Web sites are updated and often removed from the Internet, check your Bookmarks/Favorites frequently. Netscape can even do that for you. Go to **Windows>Bookmarks**. Your Bookmarks appear on the left of your screen. Go to **View>Update Bookmarks**.

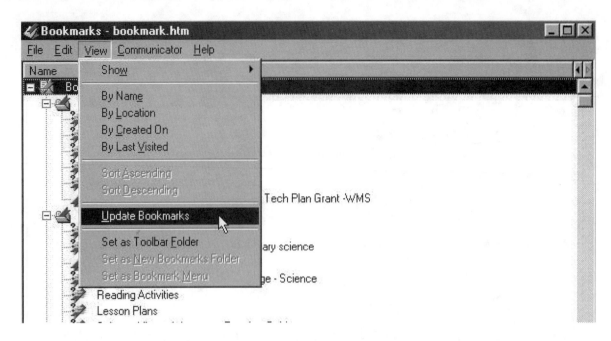

When the following screen appears, click on **All bookmarks** or **Selected Bookmarks**, and then the **Start Checking** button.

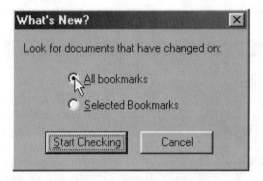

Note: Checking your bookmarks may take some time if you have a large number.

The same is possible with Internet Explorer. Follow these easy directions:
From your top menu bar, select **Tools>Synchronize** as shown below and follow the easy step-by-step directions.

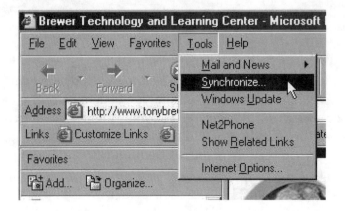

Searching the Web

At one time, searching for information on the Internet was a fairly long and tedious process, requiring you to type in various and sundry Unix commands to tell the computer what to do. Things have changed. While we still must tell the computer what to do, it is a lot less complicated. Today, we only need to have Netscape or Internet Explorer. The task is quick and easy with the aid of thousands of incredible search engines such as Google, Mamma, and AltaVista. Select a search engine, type a keyword, and within seconds your query is answered. More than 99% of the time, you can readily find the information you're seeking.

Moreover, a significant change has taken place with the new family of search engines. For the most part, we don't need to use Boolean operators, (+ or -) anymore. Instead, we can now tell the search engine exactly what we want. For example, when using AltaVista we needed to use quotation marks and + or - signs like this:

"Lesson plans" + math + "6th grade"

Below is a search for 6th grade math lesson plans using AltaVista. Notice that I have included the appropriate Boolean operators.

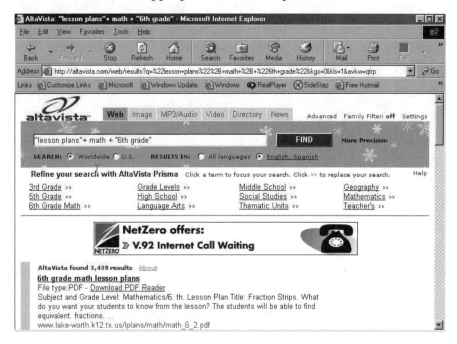

This search returned 3,439 hits. Now, let's do the same search without all the quotation marks and + or - signs.

Some search engines such as Mamma, Dogpile, and Savvy Search use many other search engine databases at the same time to look for your query.

These meta-search tools scour the databases of other search tools, select the top hits from each, throw out any duplicates, and collate the balance into an organized list.

It is important for you to know that each search tool has its own database of information. Do not rely upon any one, search tool. That is why meta-search tools are so valuable. They quickly sample the data of the other tools to save you time.

An excellent list of the major search engines by type and service and how each operates is available at: http://www.refdesk.com/newsrch.html. To get there quickly, simply type **refdesk** in your location box. This site includes links to expert advice, as well as homework helpers.

Another great next-generation search engine is Fossick. Fossick uses more than 3000 other specialized search engine databases and topical guides to search for your query, and it does not require the use of Boolean type connector words such as *and, or, not.*

Below, I have typed in a search for 8th grade earth science lesson plans:

Fossick.com - the WebSearch Alliance Directory, is a selective collection of over 3,000 specialist search engines and topical guides.

There are thousands of search engines on the Internet. Most of them can provide much more detailed searches within their specialist field than the general search engines. Fossick.com aims to help users locate the best search tools for their search needs, resulting in faster and more accurate search results.

Apart from the Fossick WebSearch Alliance Directory, our Fossick Meta Search FMS offers one of the most intelligent and advanced meta search engines available on the net today. FMS provides fast searches of the entire Net, or country-specific searches for more than 32 individual countries.

The results show 94 hits rated by the number of stars to indicate relevance.

The following screen capture shows the possibilities using Fossick. Notice you can search All the Words, Any word, or As a Phrase. The Boolean operators are built right in.

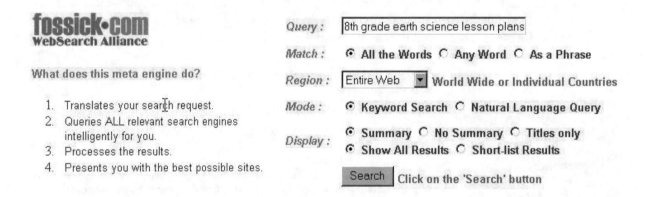

Once you have found the information you desire, you can review the information, print it out by clicking the **Print** button, or save it to a file. To save the information, select **File** from atop your browser's screen, and scroll down to **Save As**. Select where you would like to store the information from the options given and click **Save**. You may also choose to keep your search results for further exploration without having to conduct the search again. To do so, simply mark it as a Favorite or a Bookmark.

You might want to consider a Search Engine Tutorial for your students. An excellent one can be found at: http://searchenginewatch.com/resources/tutorials.html.

Searching methods vary. Find the one that works best for you and you will enjoy many minutes or hours of searching and finding information you have always wanted, but never knew where to look.

Copying and Pasting From the Internet

Essentially, there are five things your students need to learn to derive the most benefit from the Internet. Your school's Internet training program should include each of the following:

How to:
- **Use** the Internet to communicate properly;
- **Search** the Internet effectively;
- **Copy and Paste** from the Internet;
- **Sort** and **Evaluate** online resources; and
- **Cite** resources correctly.

The first two items were addressed earlier in this book. Citing online resources is addressed in Section 7 and evaluating online resources in Section 8.

Copying and pasting from the Internet is one of the most fun things you and your students will learn to do. It brings the world's resources to your doorstep with the click of a mouse. The Internet contains thousands of pieces of free clip art, images, photographs, graphics, and text that your students can use in reports, or for you to use in your thesis.

Mac and Windows machines operate slightly differently in copying and pasting, so I will be marking the distinction as we progress. Each of the individual word processing document creation software programs also complete copying and pasting differently. Neither SimpleText nor NotePad allows you to copy and paste graphics. They are both used for text only.

Copying and Pasting Text

Let us say that you want your students to find Lincoln's Gettysburg Address and copy and paste it into a word-processing document. Below are the step-by-step directions for copying and pasting it into their choice of documents. For this example, I used Microsoft Word.

1. Open the word-processing document of your choice, Word Perfect, Claris Works, Microsoft Word, etc.

2. With the word processing document open launch Netscape or Internet Explorer.

3. Search the Internet using whichever search engine you desire and locate the text you wish to copy. Click-and-hold the mouse key down while scrolling right or left over the portion of text you wish to copy; the text will be highlighted. You may also go to **Edit** and down to **Select all** from the pull-down menu if you wish to copy all the text on a given Web page. *Only* the text you select is copied to your clipboard, not images.

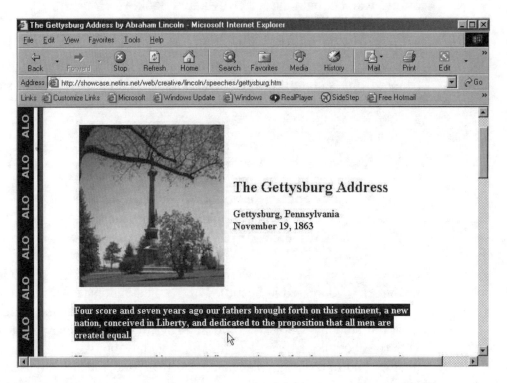

In this case, I have highlighted the first paragraph of the address only. I went to the menu bar, selected **Edit**, and scrolled down to **Copy**. This action copies the highlighted text onto my clipboard. (All computers come with a clipboard.) If you are a Windows user, right-click on the highlighted text, and then select **Copy**.

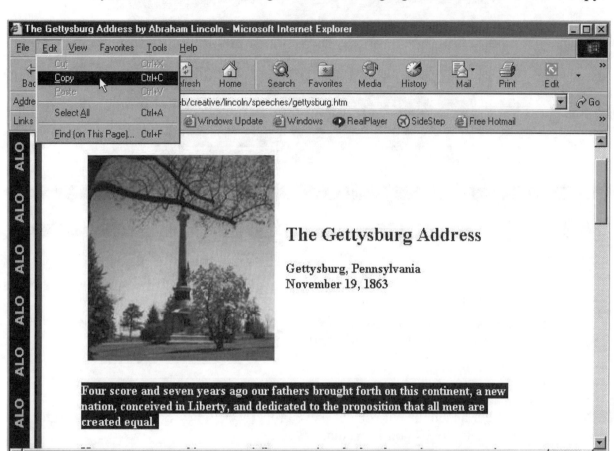

Note: Only one item may be copied to the clipboard at a time. You must paste each item of text or image before continuing to copy additional text.

4. Return to the word-processing document.

5. Position your cursor where you wish to place the text and go to **Edit>Paste** from the pull-down menu, as shown on the following page. Windows users may once again right-click and select **Paste** from the dialog box. The text you copied is transferred to the word-processing document. Once it's in the document, you can manipulate the text any way you wish; enlarge or change the font, change the color, make it bold, italic, etc.

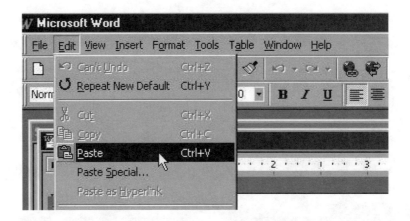

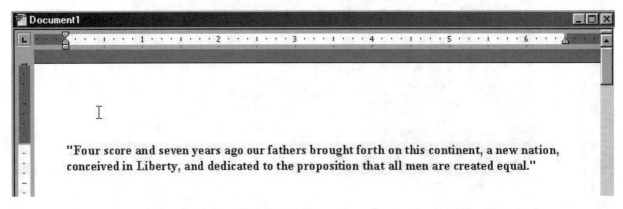

"Four score and seven years ago our fathers brought forth on this continent, a new nation, conceived in Liberty, and dedicated to the proposition that all men are created equal."

That's all there is to it. That was pretty easy, but remember that the job is not finished until your students have properly cited the resource. Be sure to have them refer to Section 7 on citing resources.

Copy and Pasting Graphics
Now, assume you want your students to locate and copy and paste a picture of the Gettysburg Battlefield from the Internet to the same document.

1. Follow the same procedure as Steps 1 and 2 for copying text.

2. Locate the desired photograph to copy and place your mouse cursor somewhere on it. Hold the mouse key down and several choices appear next to the image. **Select Copy** or **Copy this Image** from the list and release your mouse key. As in copying text, the image is transferred to your clipboard. The screen capture at right shows a picture of the Gettysburg Battlefield being copied to the clipboard.

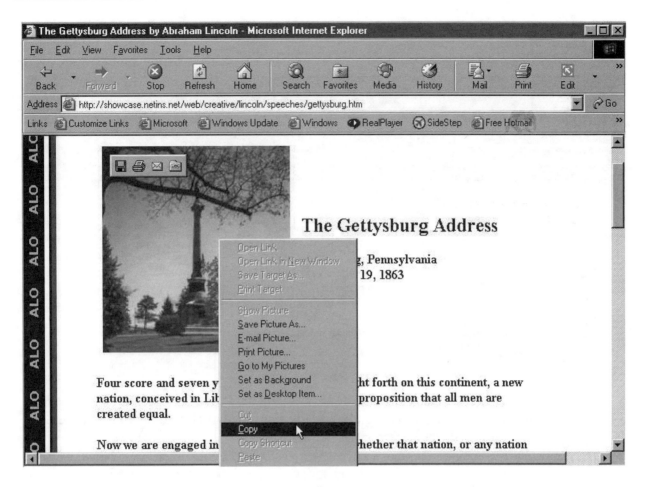

Note: To save the image into a file for later insertion into a research paper, select **Save Picture As**. Choose the file in which you wish to store the image from the choices provided, including on a floppy disk.

   MAC users hold the mouse key down on the image until the dialog box appears, and then select **Copy** or **Save.** (Or, simply click-and-drag the picture over to the desktop.)

3. Return to the word-processing document. Place your cursor where the image is to be placed in the document. Select **Edit>Paste** from the pull-down menu and the image appears on the page along with the text you have already placed there, as shown on the next page. Windows users may also right-click where they wish to place the image and select **Paste** from the dialog box.

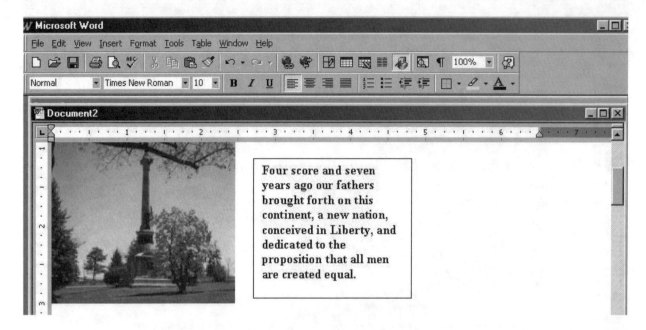

Notice that I have created a **Textbox** next to the image that allows me to place the text inside. The textbox can be expanded or contracted to rearrange the text until it fits the necessary space.

Click on the image once if you wish to resize or otherwise manipulate it. An outline appears around the image with a small box in the lower right-hand corner. Click-and-hold the mouse button down on this button and drag your mouse to make the image smaller or larger. Increasing the image size, however, tends to distort it. Clicking anywhere off of the image returns you to the document.

Some word processors allow you to click on and move the image while holding the mouse button down. You may also use the *tab*, *space*, and *return* keys to move an image.

When you have finished copying and pasting the text and images to your report, be sure to copy and paste the necessary **Online Resource Citing** information. When you are finished with the report, click **Save As** from the **File** menu. Once you have the document safely saved into a file, you can make changes as you desire. Be sure to complete a **File>Save** after making any changes.

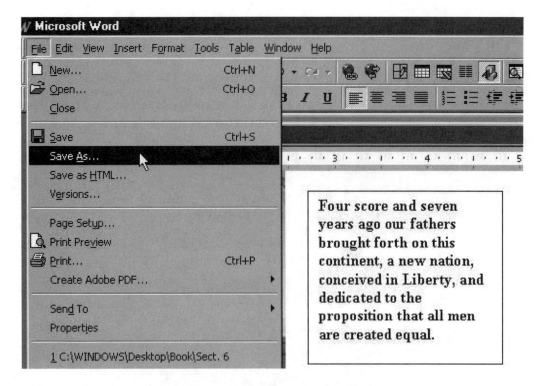

4. Once you have selected **Save Image As**, a screen appears, asking where you wish to save the image. The image will already have a name, but you can click on the filename and rename it whatever you like. The filename should be no longer than eight characters (although it can be) and end in .jpg or .gif (e.g., airplane.jpg or car.gif).

Below the filename is a box containing either **gif files**, **All files**, or **HTML Files**. Select **All files** or **HTML Files**. The image can be saved anywhere you wish, including a **floppy disk** (**A: drive**) or on the hard drive (**C: drive**.) In this example, we selected the **C: drive**. Click **OK** at the bottom of the screen. Now, scroll down and left-click on **windows**.

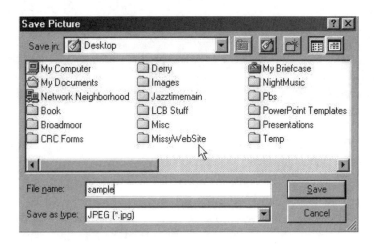

5. Click **OK** again. Now, scroll down and click on **desktop** from the new listings. Click **OK** again and the image is saved onto your desktop.

Note: You do not have to place the image into the word document now because it is not on your clipboard, but rather on the desktop or in a file somewhere you have designated.

6. Click **Insert** from the menu at the top of the screen. Scroll down and release the mouse key on **Picture>From File**.

The following inset, or something similar, appears on your screen.

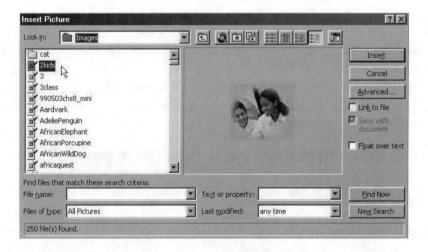

7. Select the appropriate **image filename**, which will be in the box on the left side of the large inset box. A preview of the image appears in the box on the right, as shown. Click **Insert** to the right of the image preview and the image is pasted into the word-processing document. The image may now be moved anywhere you wish in the document by clicking your mouse to the left of it and using your *tab* key, *enter* key or *spacebar*.

A small cube appears in the lower right-hand corner of the now outlined image, as well as in the center of both the vertical and horizontal lines on some machines.

Click-and-hold your mouse key down on any of these cubes to resize the image diagonally, left or right, or up or down.

While your version of Windows may not be exactly like this one, they are all similar in nature and quite intuitive. As stated earlier, some of you will be able to simply copy and paste images into certain documents, whereas others will need to follow the **Save Image As** procedure above. With a few practice sessions, you will find that copying and pasting images is fun. Your students are sure to enjoy any activity that entails the use of this feature.

Domain Names

Domain names are the last part of a URL or address. Quite often they identify the exact owner of the domain name, as in www.ford.com. We can be reasonably sure that the Ford Motor Company owns that site, but it's not always the case. Some early Internet Web designers were able to secure the domain names for famous people or companies and have made a fortune reselling them to their namesakes.

The following are some of the most common domain names:

.com   Commercial enterprises

.gov   Government agencies or offices

.mil   Military

.org   Organizations, including not-for-profits

.edu   Educational institutions

.net   Networks, like many ISPs

InterNIC, the registrar of all domain names for the Internet has been succeeded by IANA, The Internet Assigned Number Authority, which formed the Council of Registrars. This council comprises about 25 United States Internet Service Providers.

Much like the overcrowding problem of the 800 numbers in our toll-free telephone service, or the fact that the Internet is receiving too many applicants for domain names ending in the above domains, there is a demand for more extensions. More and more individuals and businesses want to be a part of the greatest technological explosion since the invention of the telephone. They are developing their own Web sites by the thousands every day.

The need for additional domain names will only increase over the next decade. The Council of Registrars has created a new list of additional domain names to help alleviate this overcrowding. Some of the new domain names include:

.firm   Businesses such as law offices, etc.

.shop   Retail operations offering goods for sale

.web   Web-related companies or individuals

.arts   Cultural- or entertainment-oriented groups

.rec   Recreational groups

.info   Groups providing informational services

.nom   Individual or personal sites

.biz   Special businesses

.tv   television affiliated sites

These new domain names were scheduled to begin appearing in 2002. You can locate a list of the Internet Service Providers who have been selected as registrars for domain names at:

www.gtld-mou.org/docs/reg-results.html

Section 6 — The Great Educator's Web Sites Tour

I have included some of my favorite World Wide Web sites for your viewing pleasure. There is something here for everyone. Regardless of your discipline area, grade level or area of special interest, the Internet is full of sites that will both amaze and stimulate your interest in using this medium to deliver content in your classrooms.

I've also included a brief description of what is available at each site. Remember, if any words, phrases, or graphics are in blue, red, yellow or green type, or are outlined in one of those colors, it is probably a hyperlink. So click on whatever you would like after accessing the site and explore. To begin, let's take a look at my Web site.

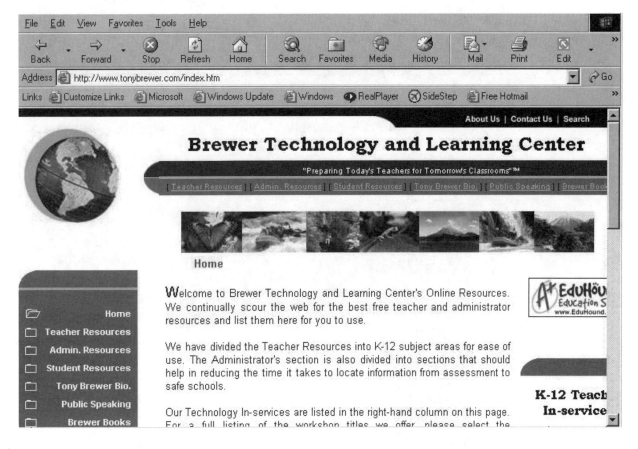

The Brewer Technology and Learning Center is dedicated to helping K–12 teachers and administrators quickly and easily locate volumes of exciting, rich, education-specific information on the Internet. From Administrator Resources to Classroom Central™ this site is a great place to start.

Be sure to visit **Ask An Expert** with your students. Experts in every field of endeavor are available 24 hours a day to answer your students' questions.

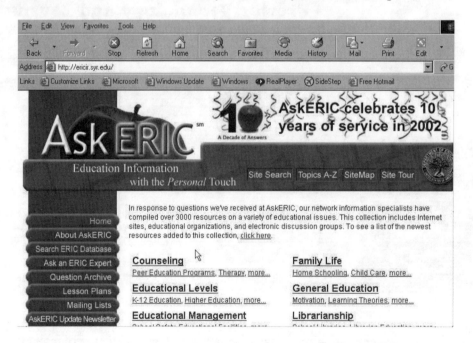

A must-see site for teachers. ERIC, the Educational Resource and Information Center located at Syracuse University is an excellent source for K–12 lesson plans.

From A to Z, this Web site is well worth the visit. Specializing in Thematic units.

Another must-visit site is Ask Jeeves™. This wonderful site allows students to ask any conceivable question.

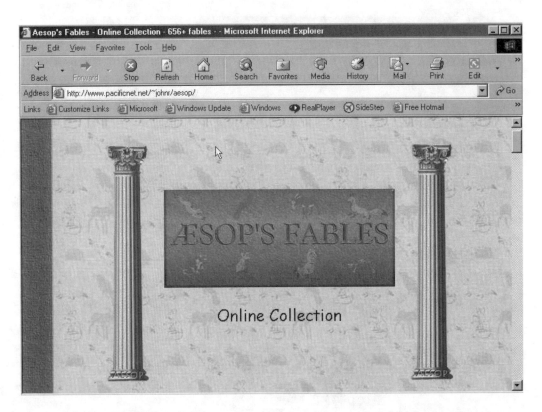

This site offers a marvelous collection of more than 200 Aesop's Fables. Sure to delight your students.

One of my personal favorites is Classroom Connect. A superb site containing everything teachers' need for professional development.

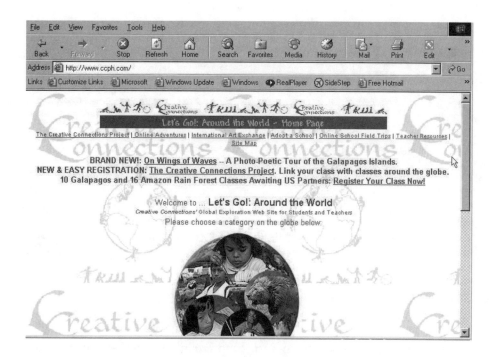

Connect your class to a class in the Amazon rain forest, Africa, China, the Arctic or the Galapagos. A recent Teachers' Favorite Site.

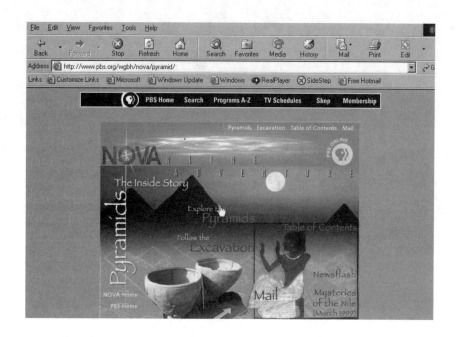

If you're interested in archaeology, check out this great site, with tons of information from Egypt and the Near East. Everyone loves the Pyramids.

Lesson Plans - Worksheets - Teacher's Lesson Plans - WebQuests - Primary Teacher Resources - Math Lesson Plans - Writing Lesson Plans - Reading Lesson Plans - Science Lesson Plans - Technology Lesson Plans - Social Studies Lesson Plans - ...

11443 Lesson Plans, **1296** WebQuests, **5000 Free Worksheet Generators, 1600 Word and Critical Thinking Problems,** Exams and Puzzles for Standardized Tests.

The spelling and vocabulary sections now include new worksheets and tools!
New Word Stories Math Problems Section!
Addition, Subtraction, Multiplication, and Division worksheets now use bigger fonts!
Language Arts Worksheets   NEW CAPITALIZATION WORKSHEETS, TOOLS, and STORIES!
New **Animal Worksheets**   Solar System Worksheets   Weather Worksheets   Plants
Reading + Math + Vocabulary + Spelling + Writing = **edHelper's New Reading Comprehension Section**
New Phonics Section with Printables and Worksheets

Christmas Stories, Math Problems, Word Search, Puzzles, and More!
Winter Theme Unit

The Ice Storm
Now Playing!

Lesson plans, worksheets, and tons more can be found at this remarkable teachers' site.

Another fantastic site especially designed for teachers—EduHound is sure to astound.

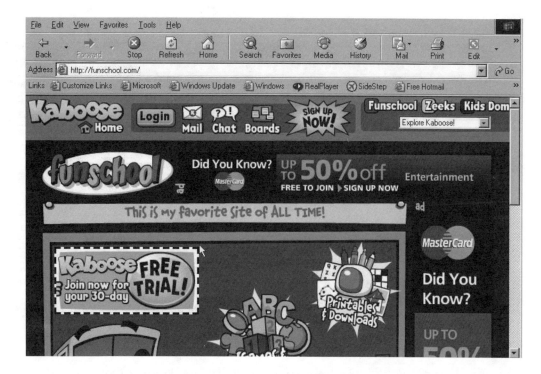

If it's games and online activities you're seeking, be sure to stop by Funschool for all the excitement and learning you and your students can stand.

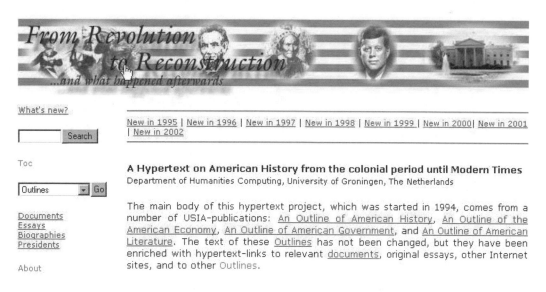

American history comes to life when taught using the Web as a vehicle for learning. Be sure to visit this very well done site.

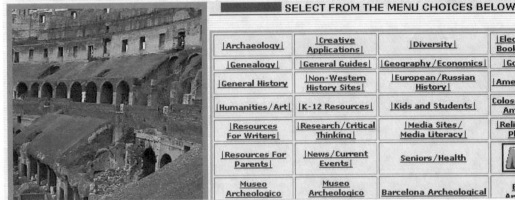

Be sure to check out this extremely useful site. Hoping that more educators will find fun, inventive ways to use the Web to deliver curriculum content, the site is especially teacher friendly.

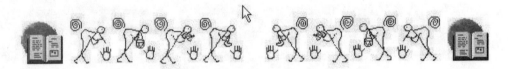

WWW Virtual Library - American Indians
Index of Native American Resources on the Internet

The World Wide Web Virtual Library features an ever-expanding index to the most far-reaching information on Native Americans found anywhere. A perfect place for students to begin researching for special projects or WebQuests.

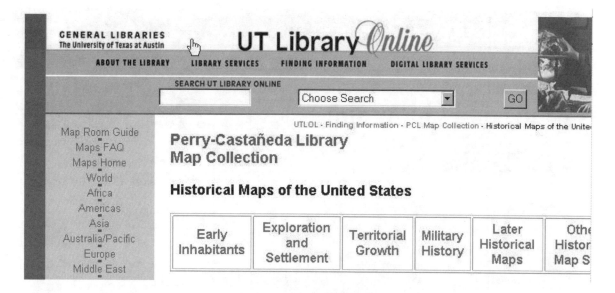

If you are looking for maps pertaining to early American history, then this is the online place for you. The site features both our earliest inhabitants and early military maps.

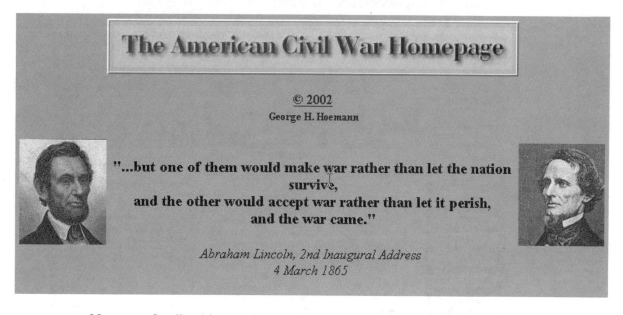

No tour of online history sites would be complete without a visit to one of the finest examples of the American Civil War information centers.

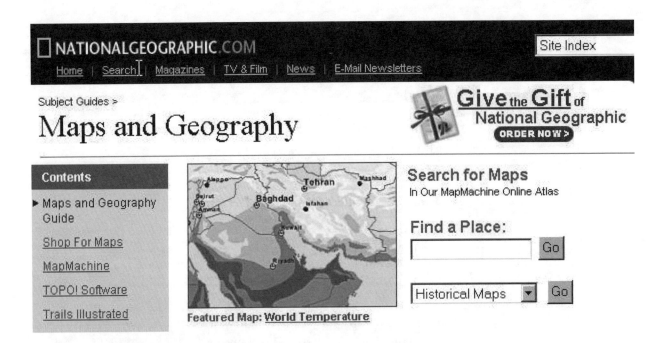

Of course, we must not overlook one of the most recognized names in American culture, National Geographic. Another tremendous map site.

Teachers from far and near flock to this site to partake of it's bountiful educational resources. Everything is easily downloadable for utmost convenience.

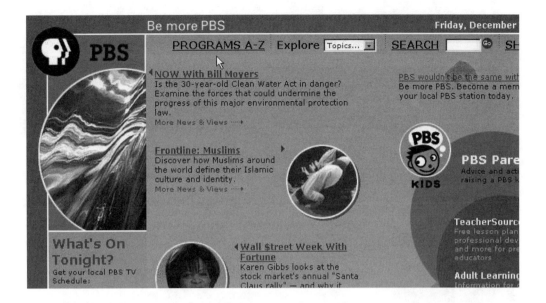

The official PBS Web site. Spending a few moments viewing the vast special programming on this site is time well spent. You will be amazed at its size.

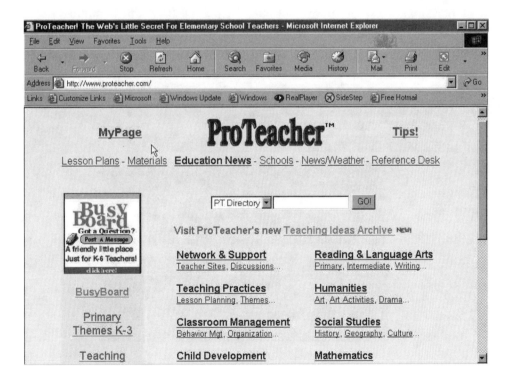

Not just another pretty face, ProTeacher is jam-packed with lesson plans, teacher resources and materials, and much more.

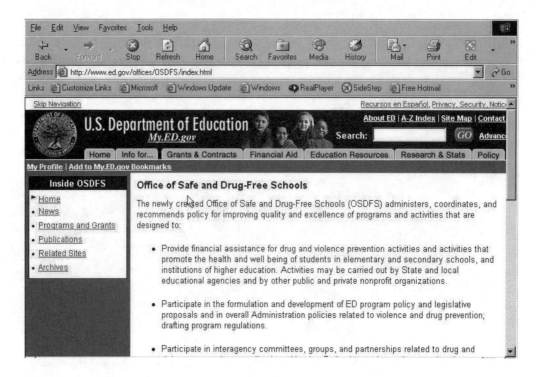

The U.S. Department of Education has put together an excellent resource pertaining to safety in our schools. You must take a few minutes to review this very useful resource.

For the early learner, this fun and exciting site is sure to help engage your students in the learning process. Its global nature opens the door to better cultural understanding.

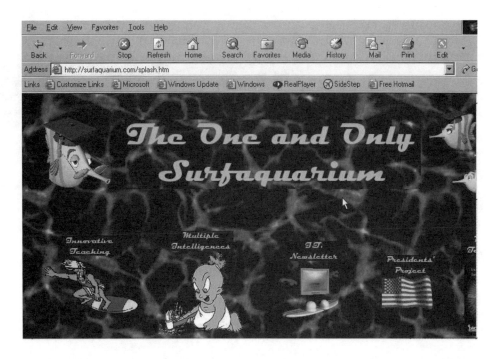

The subject of multiple intelligences comes up in every school around the world every day. This very well conceived site provides more insight into the topic than you can imagine.

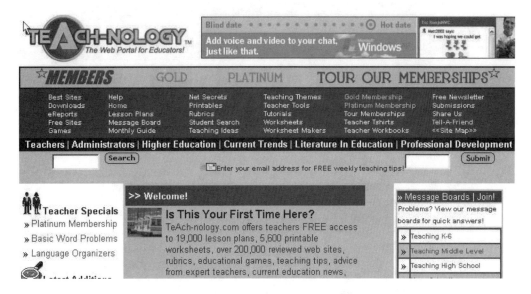

Whether you are looking for lesson plans, worksheets, rubric generators or tons of other useful teacher resources, this is the Web site for you. It focuses on K–12 classrooms.

The Visible Human Project®

NEW! **Special Announcement** NEW!

The Fourth Visible Human Project®Conference
Sponsored by the University of Colorado
Center for Human Simulation
Location: Keystone Resort, Keystone, Colorado
October 17-19, 2002

Projects Based on
the Visible Human
Data Set

Applications
for viewing
images

How much fun would it be to dissect the human anatomy? Well, maybe not particularly so in the real world; however, your students are sure to be amazed by this online learning activity.

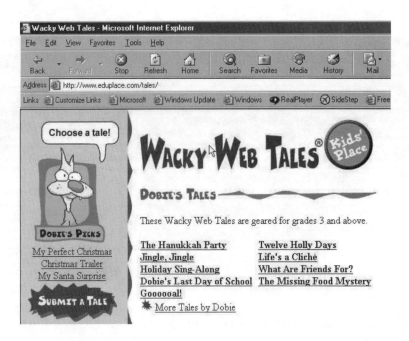

Tired of the same old humdrum? Focus on this wonderful early learner Web site. Your young charges are sure to find the stories delightful and the learning fun.

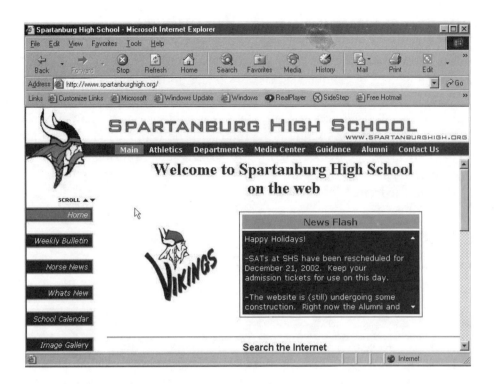

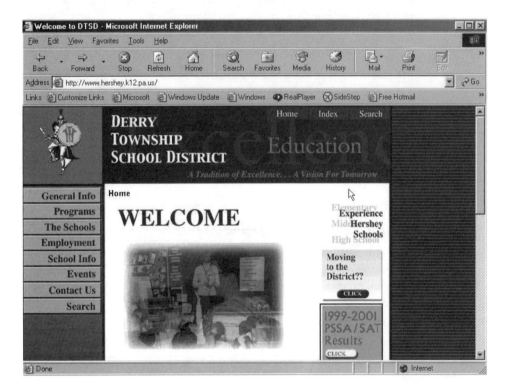

And last, but certainly not least, these two excellent school Web sites exemplify what a school or classroom can do to enhance their online presence.

Section 7 — Citing Online Resources

For most research assignments, students are required to use the school's library of encyclopedias or reference books to collect information. That information is then paraphrased and becomes the completed research paper. Students are required to include a list of references from which they obtained their data. The same holds true for information found on the Internet. The Kingswood College Library guide to citing online sources using the Modern Language Association's Style is listed below. While it is not the only source for citing online resources, I feel it covers the topic extremely well.

Kingwood College Library
Citing Online Sources
MLA STYLE

It is important to read the general rules and notes before each section. Also, keep in mind that MLA always has a five-space hanging indention.

Addiction Research Foundation. "Facts About...Alcohol."
Facts about ...Series. Toronto: Alcoholism and Drug
Addiction Research Foundation, 1991. Online. Internet. 2 Oct.
1995. Available www.io.org/~froofy/arf/facts1.txt.

Contents

General Rules for MLA Internet Citations

Please read this overview of rules that are important to the organization of your works' cited page.

Web Pages (sites or pages originally created for publication on the Internet)

Guidelines for Electronic Magazines, Journals, Newsletters, Conferences Online
     Magazine article
     Journal article
     Book review article
     Newsletter

Guidelines for Letters, Memos, e-mail Communications, Public Online Postings
     E-Mail
     Online Postings

Guidelines for Electronic Texts Online
     Book

Part of a Work
Part of a Work, FTP
Web Page
Work of Art

Guidelines for Citing Legal Sources
Public Laws
Cases/Statutes
Journal, Newsletter, News Article, Transcript

General Rules for Citing Electronic Sources

When listing an online source originally printed in a book or journal or other printed format, use the general guidelines you would use to cite the printed form. Then, follow it with information that tells where to find the source on Internet.

- Follow punctuation, capitalization, and underlining provided in the examples.
- Indent five spaces after the first line of each entry.
- Alphabetize entries by author; If no author is given, begin with title.

For more help, refer to the new *MLA Handbook for Writers of Research Papers*, 4th Ed. (rules 4.9.3 and 4.10.7)
Publication medium = [Online]
Name of computer service or network = Internet, Westlaw, Dialog, CompuServe, Prodigy
Date of access = the date you accessed the material.
Add the electronic address (URL) used to access the document. Precede the address with the word "Available." [Available http://www.nhmccd.edu/lrc/kc.]
Note: Place a period at the end of the Internet address. If you try to link to the URL, leave the period off.
Separate pieces of information by adding two spaces after each period and colon.
Most importantly, indent five spaces after the first line of each entry.

Web pages (sites or pages originally created for publication on the Internet)
Include the following:

1. Name of the author (if given; includes names of people, companies, organizations, agencies).
2. Title of the Web site or page.
3. Date of creation, publication, or copyright, or date last updated—whichever is most recent.
4. Publication medium (Online).
5. Name of person or agency maintaining this site (if given and relevant).
6. Name of the computer network (Internet).

7. Date you accessed this Web site or page. Internet address, preceded by the word "Available."

Examples

Peniche, Eduardo A. Bastogne: December 1944, White Christmas Red Snow! 1996. Online. Kingwood College Library. Internet. 7 Jan. 1997. Available www.nhmccd.cc.tx.us/lrc/kc/peniche.html.

Kunkel, Joseph G. The Cockroach Home Page: What Is a Cockroach? 3 June 1997. Online. Internet. 19 June 1997. Available www.bio.umass.edu/biology/kunkel/cockroach.html.

Paris. 1997. Online. Excite. Internet. 20 June 1997. Available www.city.net/countries/france/paris/.

Edgewood Center for Children and Families. Fragile Infant Special Care Project. 11 March 1997. Online. Internet. 15 April 1997. Available www.sirius.com/~fiscp/.

Electronic Journals, Newsletters, Conferences Online

Whether the information you use has been in printed format or not, your entry should consist of the following items:

1. Name of the author (if given)
2. Title of the article or document (in quotation marks)
3. Title of the journal, newsletter, or conference (underlined)
4. Volume number, issue number, or other identifying number (for journals only)
5. Date or year of publication (enclosed in parenthesis for journal articles)
6. Number of pages or paragraphs, or n.pag. if no page numbers are provided.
7. Publication medium [Online]
8. Name of the computer network (Internet)
9. Date you accessed the information on Internet
10. Electronic address, preceded by the word "Available"

Examples
Magazine Article
"The View from the Right Side." The Right Side of the Web 19 Sept. 1995: n. pag. Online. Internet. 14 Sept. 1995. Available www.clark.net/pub/jeffd/index.html.

Journal Article
Simon, Herbert. "Bridging the Gap: Where Cognitive Science Meets Literary Criticism." Stanford Electronic Humanities Review 4.1 (Spring 1994): n. pag.

Online. Internet. 9 Nov. 1995. Available shr.Stanford.edu/shreview/4-1/text/toc.html.

Book Review Article (See MLA 4.7.10)
Daso, Capt. Dik. Rev. of "100 Missions North: A Fighter Pilot's Story of the Vietnam War," by Brig Gen Ken Bell. <u>Air Chronicles Airpower Journal</u> (1995): n. pag. Online. Internet. 11 Nov. 1995. Available www.cdsar.af.mil/bookrev/bell.html.

Newsletter
White, Patrick. "Dutton Presents Hatfield with AAI Public Service Award." <u>American Association of Immunologists Newsletter</u> (Nov. 1995). n. pag. Online. Internet. 21 Oct. 1995. Available gopher://gopher.faseb.org:70/0./Societies/AAI/Newsletters/augsepoc195/etc/public af.

Letters, Memos, Email Communications, or Public Online Postings
(See MLA 4.10.7 for more help.)

EMail

1. Writer
2. Subject or title of document if given (enclosed in quotation marks.)
3. A description of the document that includes the recipient's name (e.g., "eMail to Peggy Whitley")
4. Date of the document

Examples
Pinkerton, Brian. WebCrawler." E-mail to Peggy Whitley". 26 Sept. 1996.

Lancashire, Ian. "email to the author." 1 Mar. 1996. [Use this form for email sent to you as author of your own paper.]

Public Posting on Electronic Network
Includes bulletin boards, commercial online services, newsgroups, or ListServs.

1. Author's name (if given)
2. Title of document (in quotation marks)
3. Date material was posted
4. Online posting
5. Name of newsgroup, listserv "delivering" the posting
6. Name of Network (Usenet, Internet)
7. Date you accessed the posting

Examples

"Special Banned Books Week Exhibit." 28 Sept. 1996. Online posting. Listserv libref-list. E-Mail. Internet. 28 Sept. 1996.

Shaumann, Thomas Michael. "Re: Technical German." 5 Aug. 1994. Online posting. Newsgroup comp.edu.languages.natural. Usenet. 7 Sept. 1995.

Books and Art Works Online

Includes Historic Documents (speeches, journals, papers) or Literary Texts (books, parts of books) on the Internet or another Computer Network. Also includes paintings, sculptures, and drawings.

1. Name of the author, if given
2. Title of part of the work, if relevant
3. Title of the painting, book, drawing, or sculpture (underlined)
4. Editor's name (books only) if given
5. Publication information for the printed source (city, publisher, date)
6. Publication medium [Online]
7. Name of the repository or agency that maintains the site where you found this material, if given. [examples: Yale, Center for Disease Control]
8. Name of the computer network [Internet]
9. Date you accessed the material
10. Electronic address, preceded by the word "Available"

Examples

Book
Austen, Jane. Pride and Prejudice. Ed. R.H. Chapman, 1994. Online. U Texas. Internet. 29 Sept. 1995. Available utx.cc.utexas.edu/~churchh/pridprej.html.

Part of a book
Blake, William. "The Marriage of Heaven and Hell." The Complete Poetry and Prose of William Black. Ed. David Bindman. Berkeley: U of California P, 1988. Online. U of Georgia. Internet. 17 June 1997. Available virtual.park.uga.edu/~wblake/eE.html.

Part of a Work, FTP [For sources that cannot be read without downloading]
Jaeckle, Peter. "Wild Boar in California: Where and How to Hunt Them." Wild Boar in California. 1994. Online. Internet. 6 Nov. 1995. Available ftp://ftp.nra.org/pub/general/ contrib/boar.txt.

Works of Art
Cassatt, Mary. Sleepy Baby. Dallas Art Museum, Dallas. Online. Internet. 2 Oct. 1995. Available gopher://gopher.unt.edu:70/g9/dfw/dma/galleries/americas/postcol/cassatt.

Legal Sources Online

We use **WESTLAW**.

Citing legal documents and law cases is complicated. Use a uniform system of citation or refer to the MLA Handbook for further assistance. Refer to the general directions for citing an online source located at the top of this document.

In general, do not underline or enclose in quotation marks titles of laws, acts, or similar documents
(Constitution of the United States).
Alphabetizing is the norm.

If you are citing the United States Code, alphabetize the entry under United States Code even though you use the USC abbreviation. If you are citing more than one code, list them by number.

Names of law cases are abbreviated (Brown v. Board of Ed.) Spell out people's names.

Public Laws

When citing an act, include the following information:

1. Name of the act [not underlined]
2. Public Law number
3. Date it was enacted
4. Statute at Large cataloging number
5. Database
6. Publication format [Online]
7. Source [Westlaw]
8. The electronic address [Available ...]

Example

Congressional Accountability Act of 1995. Pub. L. 104-1, 1995 S 2. 23 Jan. 1995. Stat. 109.3. US-PL. Online. Westlaw. Available PL 104-1, January 23, 1995, 109 Stat 3.

Cases/Statutes

When citing cases and statutes, include as much of the following information as you can find:

1. Names of the first plaintiff and the first defendant
2. Volume
3. Name (not underlined)
4. Page of the law report cited
5. Name of the court that decided the case
6. Year of the decision
7. Database
8. Publication format [Online]
9. Source [Westlaw]

10. The electronic address [Available ...]

Example
Owens v. State of TX. 875 S.W.2d 447. TX Ct. of Appeals. 1994. TX-CS. Online. Westlaw. Available 875S.W.2d 447.

Journal, newsletter, news article, television transcript
WESTLAW offers hundreds of newspapers, newsletters, journals, and radio and television full text transcripts. To cite these, use the general information and rules for online sources.

Examples
"Heart to Heart." Narr. Lesley Stahl. Sixty Minutes. CBS. 29 May 1994. 60 Minutes Online. Westlaw. Available 1994 WL3764067.

If you are writing an English paper, please check with the professor to see that you are following the guidelines of the assigned research paper. Refer to the new MLA Handbook.

The previous examples provided for you by Peggy Whitley and Catherine Olson.
MLA *Handbook for Writers of Research Papers*, 4th ed.

Section 8 — Evaluating Web Sites

Sorting the Good, the Bad, and the Ugly

For the most part, kids believe what they see on television, hear on the radio, or read in a magazine or a newspaper. Just because it's there, does not make it true. It is our responsibility as educators to help them sift through the volumes of hits (or results of searches) to point out the differences between citable and non-citable information.

Currently, no software program exists to keep students from stumbling onto non-citable resources. It takes nothing less than near-constant vigilance on the part of teachers to monitor what students are doing while online. The vast majority of schools have an *Acceptable Use Policy* that spells out expected student behavior, including treatment of hardware, software, and especially, inappropriate material they may come across. You might also include an "Internet Driver's License Program," developed by Classroom Connect, in your *Acceptable Use Policy* training.

Inappropriate content blocking software programs such as *CyberPatrol, Surfwatch,* and *NetNanny* are excellent at providing some peace of mind to nervous teachers or parents. I highly recommend them all. Nevertheless, it is supervision and monitoring that makes your children or students' time online much safer and productive. It is now easier to monitor student online behavior than ever before. Web browsers such as Netscape and Internet Explorer keep track of where your students have been. You can find the current list under the word **Go** on Netscape's menu bar, and under the small triangle at the right end of Internet Explorer's address bar. As you recall, when we set **General Preferences** earlier in the book, we could choose how many days your browser keeps track of where students have been. This is the history list.

Another excellent way to monitor student access is to type **about:global** into your location bar using Netscape. It does not work on Internet Explorer.

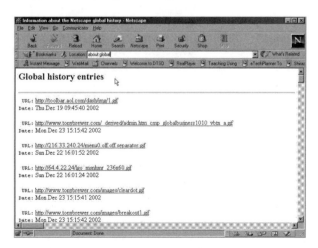

It posts a Global History List of the sites the student using a particular computer has visited on the Internet by date, hour, minute, and second. That list may then be printed out in its entirety. You may also choose to **copy and paste** only those inappropriate sites a student may have visited. This by no means is a cure-all to students reaching inappropriate material, but it will, however, give you as the teacher a way to periodically check up on their online adventures.

You may also choose to clear your **cache** of previously visited sites by clicking on **Edit/Preferences** from Netscape's top menu bar.

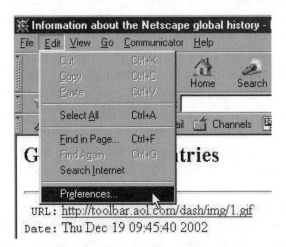

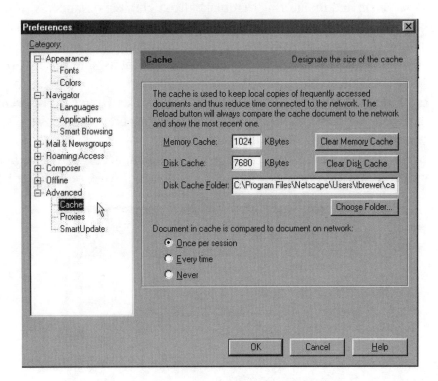

Select **Advanced/Cache**. Then, click on the **Clear Memory/Clear Disk Cache** buttons. The history disappears after you hit your **Reload** button.

Internet Explorer also provides a quick and easy way to keep track of your students' online activities. A **History** button has been placed on the Navigation bar.

Clicking on it displays a list of the most recent history, noting sites visited **Today** and **Last Week**.

Check your computer's **Temporary Internet Files** at **Tools/Internet Options/Settings.** It displays a thorough record of visited sites.

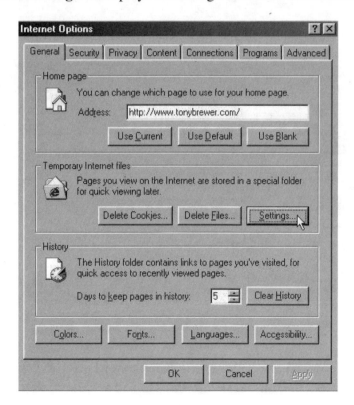

Once in the **Settings** area, click on **View Files** to display the history list.

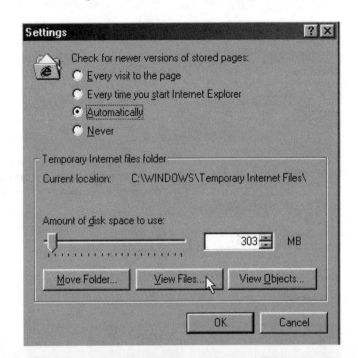

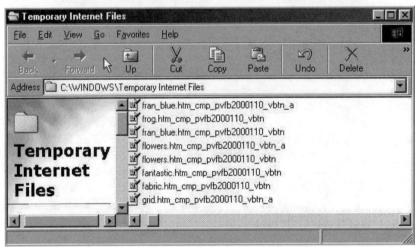

Scrolling left and right let's you view all the files.

You may also empty your **Temporary Internet Files** by going to **Tools/Internet Options/Delete Files** as shown below. Remember, you have the final say as to how your students use your classroom computers. Provide them with the tools they need to be successful in their online experiences. Students stay focused longer and function better in a more structured environment. The same holds true for integrating technology into your lessons.

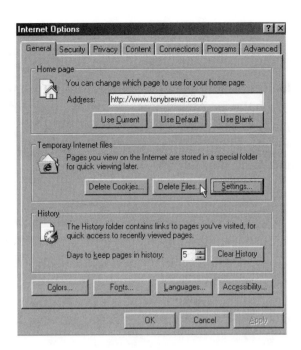

The Internet is filled with loads of outstanding, citable resources, yet finding them can sometimes be a chore. There are many excellent resources available online to help you teach your students how to properly sort bad Web sites from good ones, and I will identify them at the end of this section. There are, however, some main concepts you need to teach your students. I'll go over them briefly in this section and point you in the right direction for additional information and resources.

Sorting the Good from the Bad and Ugly

Below are some basic questions for your students to ask themselves when they begin to evaluate a Web site or other online resource. *

1. How do I begin to evaluate the quality of a Web site?

Student purpose: One of the most important criteria when evaluating a Web site is student needs. What are they using the Web for? Games, puzzles? Serious research? Most research-centered Web sites are pretty uninspiring when it comes to graphics and use of color. That, in itself, may be the reason many students overlook good, citable sources. They are often drawn to the sizzle and not always the steak. We must show students that as in life, beauty is only skin deep; it's what's hidden behind all the glitter and glitz that is of real importance. Have your students state the purpose/criteria they used for inclusion of any information from a specific Web site.

Activity: Have your students conduct a search on the Web for sites that reflect both aspects of research and glamour.

---

1. **How can I organize my approach to evaluating an online resource?**

Checklists are an excellent way to keep students organized and on task. There are many examples available online, but I have boiled it down to the lowest common denominator.

Evaluation of Web site Contents

1. **Accuracy of Web Documents**
   - Who wrote the page and can they be contacted?
   - What is the purpose of the document?
   - What is this individual's qualifications?

   Accuracy
   - Make sure author provides contact information.
   - Know the distinction between author and Webmaster.

2. **Authority of Web Documents**
   - Who published the document and is it separate from the "Webmaster?"
   - Check the domain of the document. What institution publishes this document?
   - Does the publisher list his or her qualifications?

   Authority
   - What credentials are listed for the authors?
   - Where is the document published? Check URL domain.

3. **Objectivity of Web Documents**
   - What goals/objectives does this page meet?
   - How detailed is the information?
   - What opinions (if any) are expressed by the author?

   Objectivity
   - Determine if page is a mask for advertising; if so information might be biased.
   - View any Web page as you would an infommercial on television. Ask yourself why was this written and for whom?

4. **Currency of Web Documents**
   - When was it produced?
   - When was it updated?
   - How up-to-date are the links (if any)?

Currency
- How many dead links are on the page?
- Are the links current or updated regularly?
- Is the information on the page outdated?

5. **Coverage of the Web Documents**
   - Are the links (if any) evaluated and do they complement the documents' theme?
   - Is it all images or a balance of text and images?
   - Is the information presented cited correctly?

Coverage
- If page requires special software to view the information, how much are you missing if you don't have the software?
- Is it free or is there a fee to obtain the information?
- Is there an option for text only, or frames, or a suggested browser for better viewing?

Putting it All Together

- **Accuracy:** If your page lists the author and institution that published the page and provides a way of contacting him/her.

- **Authority:** If your page lists the author credentials and its domain is preferred (.edu, .gov, .org, or .net).

- **Objectivity:** If your page provides accurate information with limited advertising and it is objective in presenting the information.

- **Currency:** If your page is current and updated regularly (as stated on the page) and the links (if any) are also up to date.

- **Coverage:** If you can view the information properly—not limited to fees, browser technology, or software requirement.

*As created by Jim Kapoun, "Teaching WEB evaluation: A guide for library instruction." 2001

In conclusion, perhaps Margaret Phillips of the UC Berkeley Library sums up the main components of proper Web site evaluation with the following:

"While most of the strategies for evaluating information can be applied to any type of resource (books, articles or Web sites), the unfiltered, free-form nature of the Web provides unique challenges in determining a Web site's appropriateness as an information source. In evaluating a Web site, these are some questions that you can ask yourself:

- Is there an author of the document? Can you determine the producer's credentials? If you cannot determine the author of the site, think twice about using it as a resource.
- Does a group or organization sponsor the site? If a group or organization sponsors it, does the group advocate a certain philosophy?
- Is there a date on the Web site? Is it up to date? If there is no date, again, think twice about using it.
- How reliable are the links? Are the links evaluated in any way?

"Students need to learn to evaluate the quality of information they find on the Web, as well as other information resources such as books, magazines, CD-ROM, and television. Ask students to be skeptical of everything they find. Encourage them to compare and contrast different information resources."

From:
Evaluating Internet Resources {Available Online,
http://eduscapes.com/tap/topic32.htm}

Section 9 — A Good Backup Plan

Web Whacking with Internet Explorer

Although we all wish we lived in a perfect world in which technology never failed, the fact is, we don't. That's why it's imperative that we have a backup lesson plan in the event of network failure. However, a software program called WebWhacker can be purchased at http://www.bluesquirrel.com. It allows you to "capture" parts of, or an entire Web site onto your computer's hard drive. The price is approximately $49.95 and a Mac version is also available.

WebWhacker 5.0 for Win 95/98/NT/2K/XP

Copy entire web sites to your hard drive.
New 5.0 is now faster and easier.

WEBWHACKER
Features
FAQ's
Support
New in 5.0
Online Manuals
Buy Now
Free Downloads
WW4.0 for MAC

If you don't wish to purchase the program, you can use the Webwhacking or **Offline Use** function of Internet Explorer. It, however, only allows you to whack three levels of a Web site. The following is the step-by-step process.

1. Launch Internet Explorer. (Netscape only allows offline work with mail and newsgroups.)

2. Navigate to the Web site you wish to whack, or the pages you wish to capture.

3. Select **Favorites>Add to Favorites** from the top menu bar as shown on the next page.

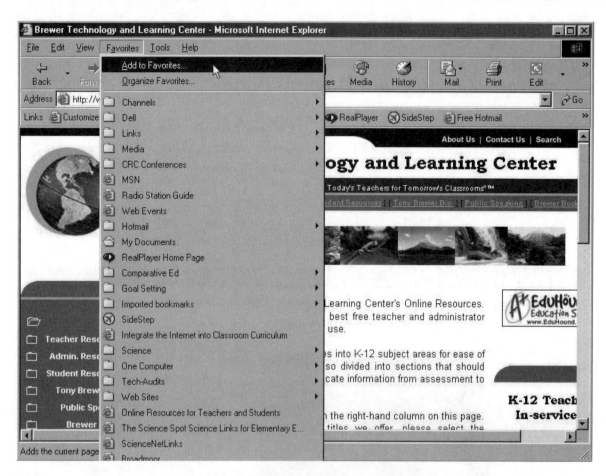

4. Before you begin whacking Web site pages, create a new folder in which to store your whackings. To do so, select the **New Folder** option as shown below.

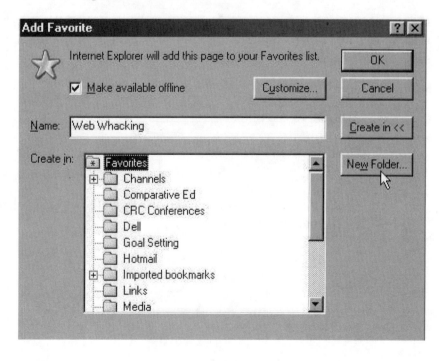

5. Type a name for the folder. I chose Lesson Plans as shown below.

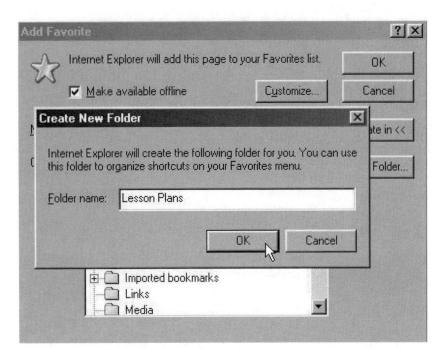

The following screen capture shows the new Lesson Plans folder we created.

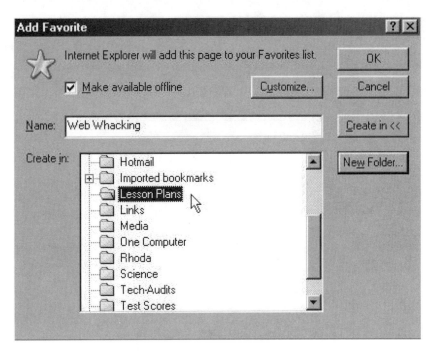

6. The name of the Web site you wish to whack appears in the **Name** box. You will, by default, be saving the site into your Favorites folder. You may choose another location, but leaving it in your

Favorites folder is probably the best place. Click in the **Make available offline** box as shown. Click **Customize**.

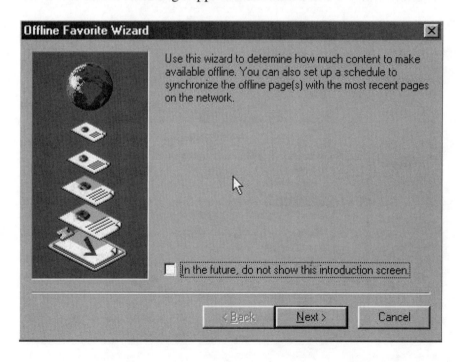

7. The next image appears. Click **Next**.

8. The next image displays the name of the site you are whacking, it's address, and asks you how many links (pages) deep you wish to capture. The **maximum** is **three**. I have chosen **two**. Click **Next** when you have made your choices.

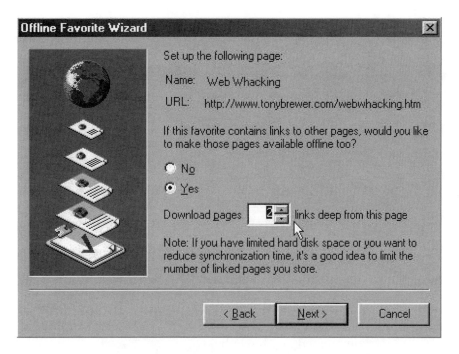

9. This screen gives you the opportunity to **Refresh** or synchronize your captured pages each time you go online. I have selected **Only when I choose**. I suggest you do the same, otherwise each time you are Internet-connected and launch your whacked sites the program automatically begins refreshing.

10. Click **Next** and you are almost finished.

11. This screen asks you if the site you are trying to capture requires a password. If it does, enter your password and user name. *Note:* Most sites that require a password don't allow you to whack them. You will receive a polite message from Internet Explorer telling you that the site doesn't wish to be whacked.

12. Click the **Finish** button and your site is whacked into the folder you created, as shown below.

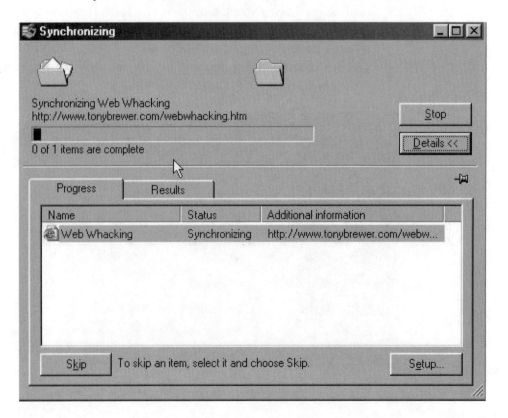

If an item appears on the screen above that you don't wish to whack, select it by clicking on that item once, and then clicking **Skip**. Remember that Internet Explorer only allows you to whack three levels deep into a Web site. Therefore, if the pages you want are levels 3 and 4, you can start your whack on level 3. Or, you can whack the first three levels, and than the next two, and so on.

Section 10 — Internet Lesson Plans

What are Internet Lesson Plans?

Essentially, Internet lesson plans are the same lesson plans you currently use, with one additional ingredient—technology. They often, and preferably, cross discipline boundaries allowing students to experience the world around them in a completely new light. Much like thematic units, they encourage and invite students to explore beyond the original lesson plan intent.

Studying about Christopher Columbus can be much more than a social studies or history lesson. It might include mathematics—how many days would it take to cross the Atlantic Ocean, a distance of approximately 3,000 miles, traveling at an average speed of seven knots per hour? How about science? Why not download storm-tracking software from N.O.A.A. and learn to predict the best time of year for Columbus to set sail?

Why not learn a foreign language at the same time? Current software is available that allows students to communicate via email with a group of peers living in Spain. Students type their questions in English and the software automatically converts it into Spanish. When the students in Spain reply, the translation takes place in reverse. Now, we're not only talking about learning a foreign language, but how students can learn to type, spell, and communicate like never before. Students experience multiculturalism first hand.

Certainly, communicating with someone in a foreign country via email is not the same as being there, but it might possibly excite and inspire some of your students to actually visit that distant peer someday. Einstein once said, "Imagination is more important than knowledge." If we can find some way to excite the natural curiosity in our students, the learning really begins to take place.

Technology, like the Internet, can and is proving to be an excellent source for just such motivation. Many recent studies on the efficacy of integrating technology into the classroom confirm that remarkable improvements are being noted in all academic areas, including the area of special education. As we are acutely aware, motivating students today can be a difficult task.

Last spring in Huntington Beach, California, I presented an all-day seminar on the basics of the Internet. Because I address such issues as pornography and how to properly monitor a child's online excursions the class is usually reserved for adults. However, shortly before the beginning of class, a 13-year old boy entered the room and took the only remaining seat, which happened to be in the front row. He was wearing an imitation surfing wetsuit and had 4-inch long, blond, spiked hair held straight up with butcher's wax. It was flat across the top, much like kids wore back in the wild and crazy sixties. I asked him why he was here and he replied, "My dad was supposed to be here, but he got sick and couldn't make it. He said he'd paid a lot of money to hear you speak and somebody was going, so here I am!"

"Great," I said as excitedly as I could without sounding contrite. "I'm glad to have you here. Do you like school? " I asked.

"No way, Dude," he unashamedly pronounced.

"Why not?" I just as unashamedly inquired.

"Cause it's boring," he asserted. "It's the same old thing day after day, nothing ever changes."

"Well then, you must like computers," I offered, feeling a little guilty for ignoring the rest of the audience.

"Not a chance Dude," he immediately countered, "They're stupid!"

"So," I dared to ask. "What do you like to do then?"

"Surf dude," he replied, in a voice loud enough for the folks three floors up to hear.

"Cool," I said. "Real cool."

Well, needless to say, I figured this was going to be a long day. For the next hour and a half, he pretended he was being held captive by aliens from another planet. He used up every inch of the limited space the ladies on either side provided and bolted from the room like he was shot from a cannon at the morning break. I wondered if he'd come back for the rest of the day.

He had hardly left the room when I began "surfing" the Internet and downloaded a two-minute video of some "dudes" surfing in Hawaii. I had it playing on the large projection screen when he re-entered the room. I watched him carefully as he took his seat with a colossal sigh. He finally lifted his head and his eyes fell upon the screen. "Coooool," he exclaimed as he climbed over the table to get to the computer I was using.

From that moment on, this young, 13-year old was the most attentive person in the room. He even spent his entire lunch hour with me at the podium browsing the Internet for any and all references to surfing, including sending an email message to the Hawaiian Professional Surfers Association. At the end of the day I asked him if he still thought computers were stupid.

"No way, Dude," he assured me. "They're like the coolest!"

Granted, not all students react as this one did, but if you can discover something a child really enjoys and show it to him on the Internet, you'll have piqued their curiosity like never before. Even kids plagued with ADD and ADHD have become more focused for longer periods of time with the aid of technology. Technology holds a strange fascination for all of us, even among those intimidated by it. It does not matter what a child intends to do as a vocation, sooner or later they will be required to understand and use technology. It is our specific responsibility as educators to provide lesson plans and projects that integrate the use of technology along with traditional resources found in the school's library or in textbooks. Learning in the future is going to be much more of a self-guided effort, with the onus being placed more heavily on the student, allowing the teachers to become more of a guide.

Internet lesson plans are regular lesson plans that require students to add online research as one more ingredient. Sometimes, students need to communicate with experts from around the world at Web sites such as www.askanexpert.com. An expert from Astronomy to Zoology is ready and willing to answer your student's questions. Knowing the identity and credentials of that expert is extremely important, however. The experts at this Web site are all citable in their respective fields. (see citing online resources in Section 7.)

Students partner with other classes to complete joint projects or lessons, exchange information, and reach shared conclusions. They create supportive spreadsheets, graphs, and charts that show the results of their online lessons and publish them to the Internet. Students learn to do collaborative problem solving, work in teams, and exercise higher-level thinking skills. As a result of doing online searches for supportive information they increase their information literacy as well. The information found in your school library is an excellent traditional resource, and students still need to know how to access and use those resources. However, technology allows students to go beyond the school walls to retrieve the latest information from around the planet in a matter of seconds. The latter needs to compliment the former.

The ideal Internet lesson plan, like the traditional, should include: *objectives, materials needed, procedures*, and an *assessment* of a student's knowledge gain. In an Internet lesson plan, we need to include activities that integrate the use of technology.

Under ***Objectives***, we add: To gain an understanding of the use of email, or the World Wide Web as an effective communication, data collection, and research tool. It can include any or all of the new technologies.

Under ***Materials Needed***, list both Internet and non-Internet materials. Don't forget traditional resources such as your school library.

Under ***Procedures***, students are required to use those technology tools in addition to the traditional school library resources, or their textbooks to research or read about a particular topic. Be sure to give your students a place to start when introducing them to the Internet. You will need to research the topics you assign prior to doing so to give them an idea of where to start looking.

For example, if you are doing a unit on the Civil War, you may want to direct them to the Civil War Home page on the World Wide Web. Give them the address or URL (uniform resource locator) and tell them to then locate, via searching, three other sites containing citable information about the topic. Be sure to have them cite the resources they find, as they would traditional ones.

Under *Assessment*, add such things as: Were the students able to locate information on the Internet? How did they evaluate the information? Did the online research enhance their Internet skills? In addition, state what you want your students to learn, infusing both the traditional and the Internet into your lesson plans. Be sure to design an assessment rubric that fully illustrates what you expect of your students. Two excellent World Wide Web sites for designing assessment rubrics can be found at:

> **http://www.tonybrewer.com/teacher_links.htm**
> Click on **Creating Rubrics**.

> **http://teach-nology.com/web_tools/rubrics/**
> Includes a list of great Rubric generators.

Finding Lesson Plans Online

If you are having difficulty creating lesson plans for a particular area of study, there are literally thousands of lesson plans online that educators like yourself have generously contributed free of charge.

Probably the best place to start a search for appropriate lesson plans is at the Educational Research Information Center (ERIC) located on Syracuse University's Web site (ericir.syr.edu).

This Web site contains a collection of subject-specific lesson plans from around the globe, and it is searchable. Each lesson plan is easily printed out, saved to a file that you have labeled "Lesson Plans" on your hard drive, or stored on a floppy disk. Each plan includes the name of the author along with their educational affiliation, and follows the same basic format I described in the previous section.

You may also wish to visit the **Site map** (at the top of the home page); it directs you to the **Television Companion Materials** section. Here, you can use programming from the History Channel, CNN, the Discovery Channel, and many more to help teach your classes. We visit this site later in this section.

During a recent visit to ERIC in search of lesson plans I captured screenshots and have them arranged here in step-by-step order.

1. First, I opened my browser. Again, you may choose either Netscape or Internet Explorer, as they both work practically the same. I typed in the URL for ERIC (ericir.syr.edu) and pressed the *Return* or *Enter* key.

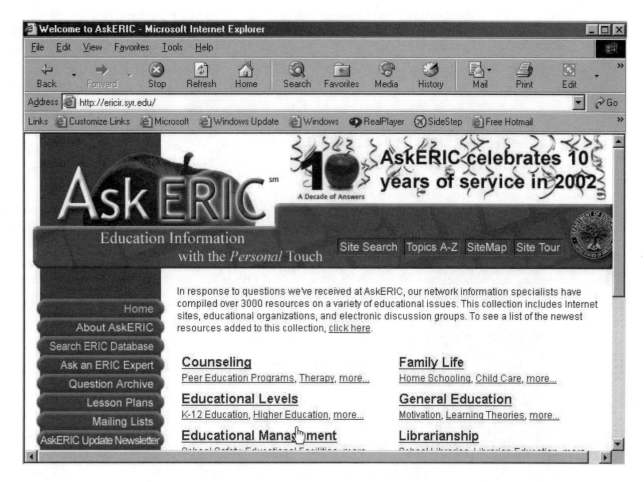

2. As you see above, the AskERIC Web site appears onscreen with an assortment of hyperlinked icons ranging from *About AskERIC* to Lesson Plans. To select an item, place your cursor on the icon you wish and click the mouse button. You can search the database, ask an ERIC Expert a question, or visit their Mailing Lists resources. Spend some time familiarizing yourself with the features AskERIC provides. There are times when they will come in handy.

3. To search for lesson plans, select the **Lesson Plans** link and click the mouse key once. AskERIC's database contains more than 2,000 unique lesson plans that cross all discipline areas.

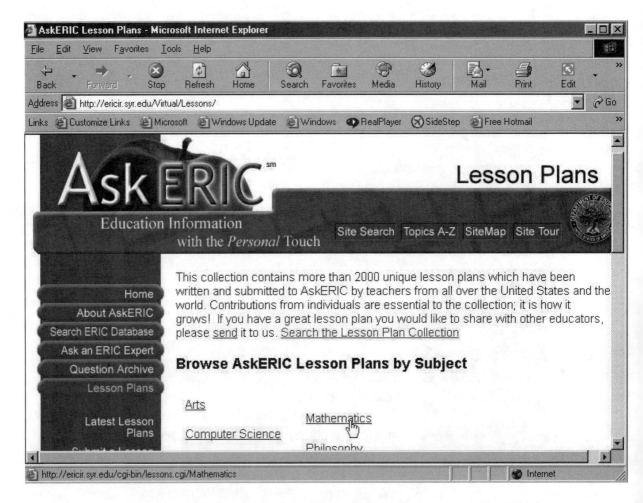

4. The above screen appears on your computer's monitor, providing you with an entirely new list of discipline area choices. AskERIC also has a link that takes you to the **Latest Lesson Plans** section where the most recently received lesson plans are listed. This list is also divided into specific discipline areas with the date of publication noted. As you can see, the Web site is quite intuitive.

5. Click your mouse on the **Mathematics** icon. As you can see on the next page, AskERIC has returned a variety of lesson plans dealing with Mathematics. It even has suggested grade levels.

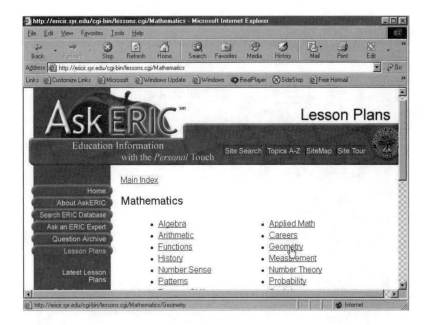

6. Select *Geometry* from the list provided. A wonderful list of **Geometry** Lesson Plans, with the appropriate grade level indicated to the right of each lesson plan, is shown. Select **Measuring the Earth** for grades 9–12.

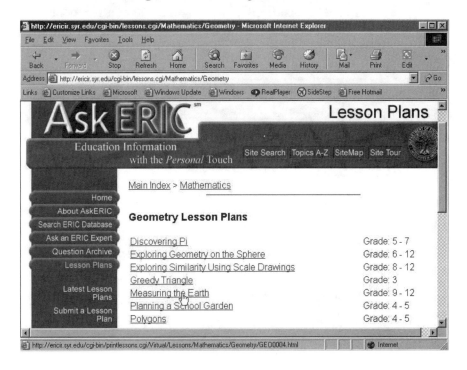

7. Below is the Lesson Plan we selected. It lists the authors name, school affiliation, and covers all the necessary steps in making the plan work in your classroom.

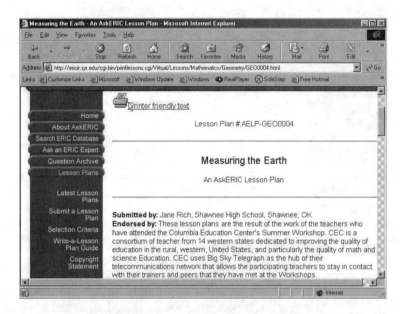

8. It may take you a while to cull through all the possible lesson plans found on AskERIC, but the time and energy spent will be well rewarded. You may also choose to search through the lesson plans for specific titles.

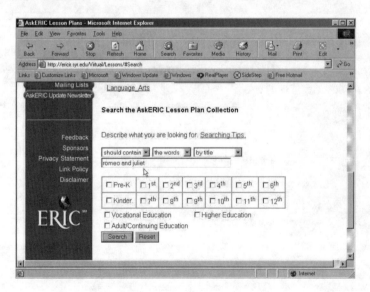

Below is a search for Romeo and Juliet lesson plans. Click on the **Search link** and type "Romeo and Juliet." Leave the grade level blank to cover the full spectrum of possibilities. As you can see, AskERIC has 272 Romeo and Juliet lessons in its database.

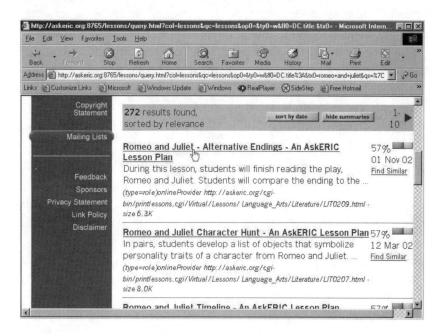

Now, click on the first lesson plan, **Romeo and Juliet - Alternative Endings**.

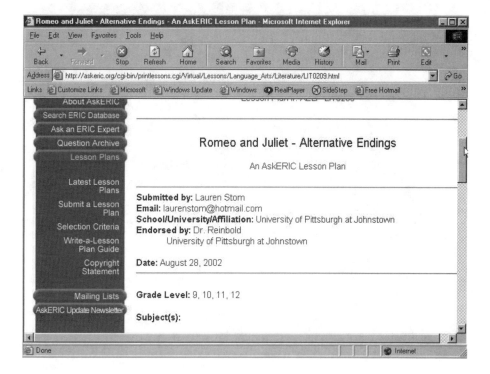

As you can see, this lesson shows when and where it was created, who created it, and the suggested grade levels.

Teachers, who wish to share their most successful plans with other teachers, submit the lesson plans. You can do the same by sending your favorite lesson plans to AskERIC. See their home page for instructions.

Once you have found a Lesson Plan and decided to try it out, you can either save it to a floppy disk, to your desktop, or into a folder you titled "Lessons."

You can also click on your browser's **Print** button and print out a hard copy. Once you have decided where you are going to save your lesson, follow the procedures for saving specifically for your computer. It doesn't matter where you save your lesson plans; it only matters that you remember where you saved them.

You may also choose to visit the additional resource area on the AskERIC Web site mentioned earlier. Navigate back to the home page and click the mouse on **SiteMap**.

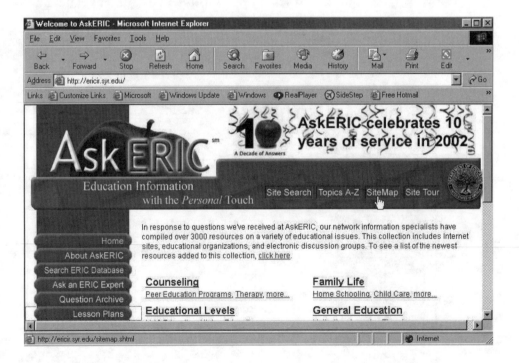

Select **Television Series Companion Materials** from the list.

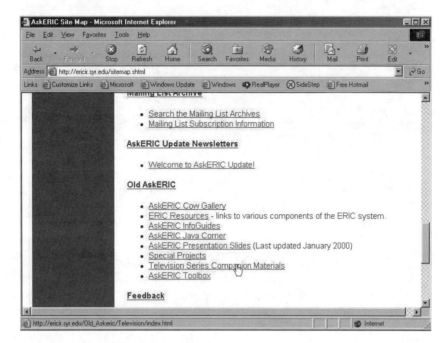

Your screen looks like the one below. Click the mouse on **A&E Classroom**.

Select **Teaching Materials** or **Classroom Tips** and off you go.

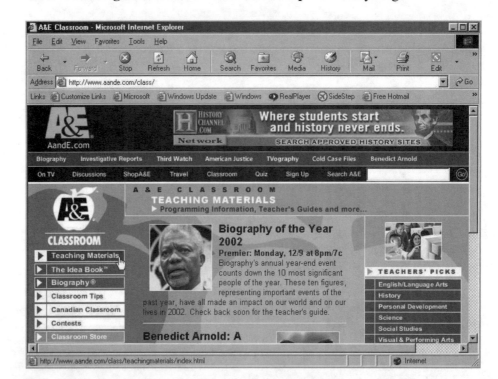

You can spend much more time at AskERIC than I did here, but I believe you probably get the idea that it is a great teacher resource. All the lesson plans here are provided for your use free of charge. It's teachers helping teachers become better teachers.

Searching for Lesson Plans Online

If you have exhausted yourself at ERIC you may want to try an Internet search.

I am going to use a Web search tool called Fossick (http://www.fossick.com) to conduct this search because of the way it ties words together without using +'s (plus signs) and -'s (minus signs). The plus sign stands for "and." The minus sign stands for "not."

Though Boolean operators still have their place in searching specific databases, it is no longer necessary for the majority of online searches conducted. In the old days (two years ago), an example of a Boolean search would be: I want information on (cats-"broadway plays") We want data on "Cats," the four-legged variety, not on Broadway plays named "Cats." Or, perhaps you want (fairy tales-dragons). In this case, we don't want any fairy tales containing dragons because they may frighten the young audience we are addressing.

Note that each search tool has it's own database of information on a wide range of topics. Some may have more data on one topic than another and vice versa. So, try not to get in the habit of using only one search tool. I recommend, as mentioned in the section on searching, that you use a meta-search tool such as **Fossick** or **Vivisimo** to do a precursory search of the Internet because it uses many search engines at once. It brings back only the top hits from each search tool, and collates them in order according to nearness to your query. It also tells you the search engine source of the references it found, with the search tool also shown as a hyperlink.

Altavista and Google are still excellent search engines. They allow us to group keywords together using Quotation "..."marks. For example, if you are looking for very specific lesson plans, you might type in the query box: "Lesson Plans"+"Language arts"+ "grade 7."

We conduct searches in this way to reduce the number of unrelated hits we receive. If I had simply typed in "lesson plans," I would receive thousands of hits. However, each time I add a keyword the search tool finds fewer and fewer references where all the keywords appear together. With Altavista, two or more keywords used together require quotation marks. One word does not.

Each search tool has its own way of searching. You should familiarize yourself with each one that you use. Most do not require the use of quotation marks or plus and minus signs. Metacrawler, for example, asks if you wish to search **Any of the words**, for **all the words**, or **As a phrase**, somewhat in the way of Boolean logic.

The following sample search for lesson plans was made using the **Google.com** search engine. Most of the Meta search engines operate much the same, so take your pick.

To begin, launch your browser. Next, type "Google.com" in the location box at the top of the page. Don't insert any spaces in the address; It won't work correctly with them.

Our search begins on the following page.

I have opened my browser and typed in the URL or address for **Google.com**. Next, I typed the words "lesson plans" in the search box. Notice that the words are lowercase and inside quotation marks. While upper- or lowercase can affect a search, it generally does not matter.

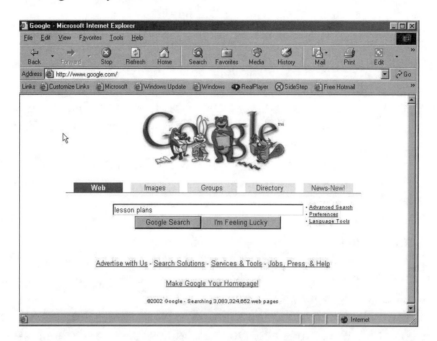

I check to see if my spelling is correct, and then click the **Google Search** button below the search box.

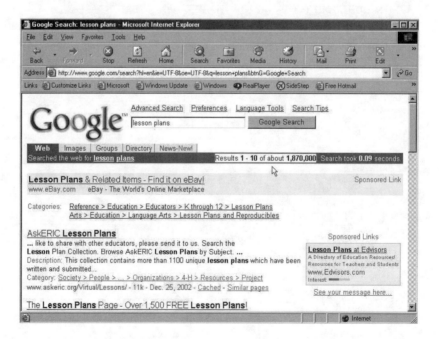

Google returned about 1,870,000 hits. The returned hits may only be references to other resources, not actually what you want. Generally speaking, the first 10–20

hits you receive will be most closely related to your keywords. Desiring to refine my search, I have added a specific discipline area, in this case, history.

Now we are getting somewhere. We've reduced the number of hits to 886,000. So, let's add a grade level.

Interestingly enough, the addition of the words history and 8th grade decreased the number of hits to just over 20,000. But, what we really want is 8th grade Civil War history lesson plans. So, let's try **removing history**, because it would be redundant, and try adding **civil war**.

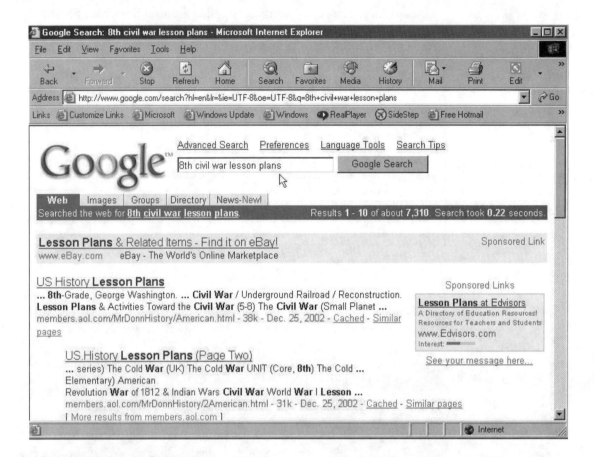

Now, that's better. We have finally reached a relatively reasonable number of hits with which to deal. Remember that of the 7310 hits returned, probably the first 10 or 20 have the best results. You will notice a series of numbers and the word **next** at the bottom of the page. It lists the additional pages of results.

As you may not be aware, you can indeed bookmark your favorite search results. That way, you won't need to redo the search each time you begin looking for new lesson plans. After you have launched a book-marked favorite, remember to hit the **Refresh** or **Reload** button to synchronize it with any new data that may have been posted since your last visit to the bookmark.

Now, let's do the same search, only this time we will use the search engine **Fossick.com**. As shown on the next page, I've typed in the same keywords, 8th grade civil war lesson plans.

Fossick returned 99 hits, reflecting exactly what we desired.

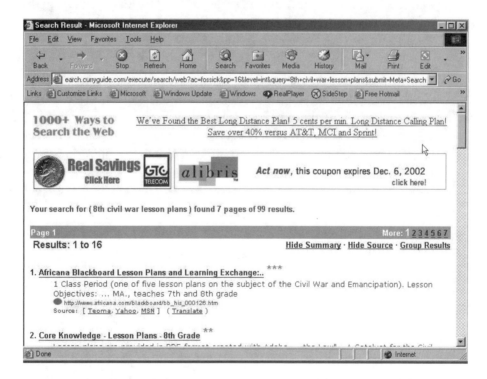

That is about all there is to searching for lesson plans on the Internet. Quite often, a search will provide hyperlinks to an additional cache of lesson plans. Be sure to bookmark your favorites whenever you come across a site that has a lot of potential. See page 61 for a list of my favorites.

Creating Your Own Internet Lesson Plans

To get you thinking in "Internet mode," I have included a template for creating an Internet Lesson Plan. If you feel this template helps as a cognitive organizer, please feel free to photocopy and reuse it as often as you like.

Realizing that you are fully aware of how to create lesson plans, I'll try to avoid overstating the obvious. Instead, I will focus on how technology can be integrated to compliment your existing lessons.

Objectives

What is it that you want your students to learn? What special skills do you want enhanced by using technology such as the Internet, or word processing software such as Microsoft Word or Word Perfect in your lesson? Does your lesson plan comply with curriculum guidelines established by your school or district?

Materials

What materials will your students need to accomplish the expectations of this lesson plan? Do your students have adequate access to the Internet to properly complete the lesson? Do you have the necessary equipment and lab time to teach your students how to use the necessary Internet tools such as email and the Web? Does your lesson require the creation of a multimedia presentation using PowerPoint or some other presentation software?

Procedures and Activities

Integrating technology applications such as communicating with experts from around the world or with peers using email, Web searching, and HTML authoring can greatly enhance the value of any given lesson plan. Be sure to check out Internet sites you recommend to your students before allotting their online time. Have your students cite their online sources properly and monitor their online time. It is quite possible for any child to monopolize the keyboard, so be sure there is some type of per-student online time checker or schedule in place.

Assessment Rubric

How will you assess the results of your students' online experiences? What methods of measurement will you employ? Will you require a written research report or have your students create a group multimedia presentation? Have they cited online resources correctly? Did they demonstrate proper use of online search tools? Were they able to successfully separate the good information from the questionable? If so, how was it done? Did your students make good use of traditional research resources in the school library? Did they compare and contrast traditional and technology derived resources? If required by your lesson plan, were students able to properly create charts, graphs, or spreadsheets? Following on the next page is an excellent free online rubric-creating program.

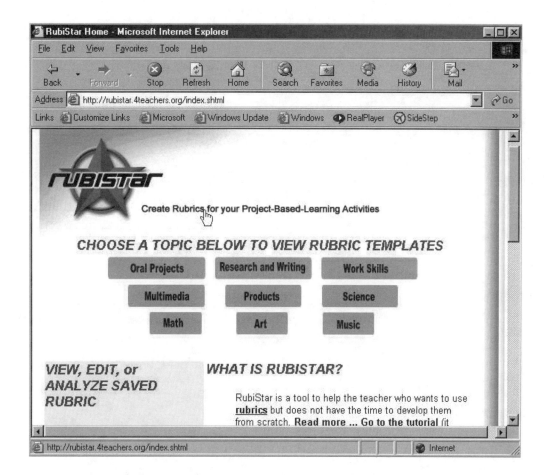

The **Lesson Plan Worksheet Template** on the following page is intended to be a guide to help organize your thoughts as you begin to integrate technology into your lesson plans. Don't be afraid to take some risks when considering what online activities to have your class complete. Try to remember that the journey is often more important than the final destination.

Internet Lesson Plan Worksheet

Objectives:

_____
_____
_____
_____
_____
_____
_____

Materials:

_____
_____
_____
_____
_____

Procedures/Activities:

_____
_____
_____
_____
_____
_____
_____
_____

Assessments/Rubric Descriptions

_____
_____
_____
_____
_____
_____

Section 11 — Internet Classroom Projects

What are Internet Projects?

An Internet project is an organized, structured online activity used to enhance the learning process through the use of technology such as the Internet, multimedia, email, and the World Wide Web.

Types of Internet Projects

Three basic types of Internet projects include Interpersonal Communications, Data Collection, and Collaborative Problem Solving. Each type has its own particular method of employing various functions within the framework of technology. Let's look at each individually.

Interpersonal Communications

This type of Internet project is usually the best and easiest way to introduce your students to the Internet. It requires them to learn how to use email as a communication tool. It works especially well with the introduction of electronic PenPals, or KeyPals. It is also the fastest way to communicate with a wide variety of experts around the world.

Data Collection

As the name implies, this type of Internet project requires students to collect data via the Internet using email, the World Wide Web, or any combination of the two. Once students have retrieved the data, they are required to integrate the data into some form of word processing chart, graph, or spreadsheet. They are then required to draw certain conclusions from the data in relation to the intended lesson plan(s) created to achieve the projects successful conclusion.

Collaborative Problem Solving

In this type of Internet project, students are given a problem or task involving a question, and are required to use the skills learned by doing the first two types of projects to reach a shared conclusion. This is the most difficult of the three types of Internet projects. It requires not only communication using email, but also considerable in-depth Internet searching and asking others around the county, state, continent, or world to provide data that can be used to arrive at a solution(s) to the stated problem or question. Requiring considerable data entry, as well as the creation of graphs, charts, or spreadsheets, this type of project is typically best when conducted using small teams. This type of project may also be better served when shared at its conclusion as a small team multimedia presentation, possibly using PowerPoint or some other presentation software. You may also wish to incorporate Scavenger Hunts into this type of project.

Because Collaborative Problem Solving can become overwhelming very quickly if not properly planned and executed and consumes much more of your and your student's time, it should probably not be the first type of project you attempt.

A fourth type of Internet project, called **WebQuests** is addressed separately in Section 12.

Finding Internet Projects Online

There are many ways to find out about ongoing, classroom designed, Internet projects. They can be found by doing Keyword Internet searches, or by joining a mailing list or two that specialize in classroom projects.

Several excellent, ongoing global projects include **MayaQuest** and **AfricaQuest**. Some charge a fee for the educational materials they supply for your students, while others do not. For a nominal fee, MayaQuest allows students to follow along in an adventure to Central America, where the explorers actually bicycle through the jungles looking for reasons for the demise of the Mayan culture, as well as studying the effects of deforestation of the rain forest. It is an exciting and educational journey that promotes student participation through email and printed materials.

If, however, you have limited funds for cyberspace exploration, there are many great projects that don't require a fee, such as **Signs of Spring**, a global data collection project, or **Where on the globe is Roger?** which is more of an email-type project.

Almost certainly, the best and easiest way to locate ongoing projects is to join a Mailing List. Several excellent lists are available, and they are only an email message away. I recommend you start by joining **IECC**, the International email Classroom Connections mailing list. It is a giant cyberspace warehouse for Internet projects.

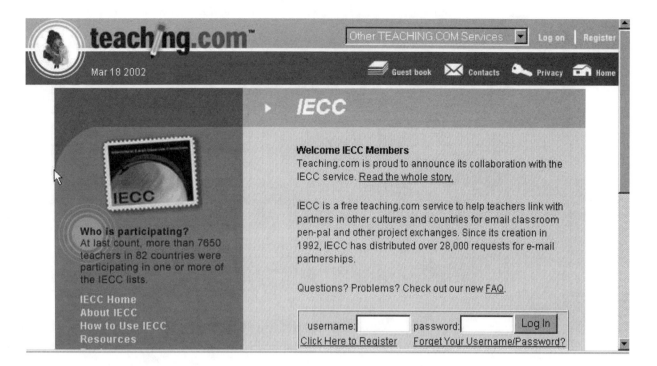

To join, visit their Web site at: http://www.iecc.org/ Be sure to check out their very nicely done FAQ section, as well as the Special Resources section. All activity at I.E.C.C. is conducted using e-mail, so your students can practice the communication portion of the foundations of technology integration discussed earlier in the book.

You might also wish to join **HILITES**, another excellent source of ongoing and archived projects. You will need to join this free mailing list to post your requests for project partners. To subscribe, visit http://www.gsn.org.

There is no fee to join the vast majority of Mailing Lists and you will find them useful in classroom activities planning. They are developed and maintained by educators like you, who want to share their knowledge and experiences.

As mentioned earlier, the other way to find projects is by conducting Internet searches. As in the section on lesson plans, this can be accomplished best by searching the Web. I will use Fossick.com again to do a sample search. I've typed in "Internet projects."

Fossick.com - the WebSearch Alliance Directory, is a selective collection of over 3,000 specialist search engines and topical guides.

There are thousands of search engines on the Internet. Most of them can provide much more detailed searches within their specialist field than the general search engines. Fossick.com aims to help users locate the best search tools for their search needs, resulting in faster and more accurate search results.

Apart from the Fossick WebSearch Alliance Directory, our Fossick Meta Search **FMS** offers one of the most intelligent and advanced meta search engines available on the net today. FMS provides fast searches of the entire Net, or country-specific searches for more than 32 individual countries.

As with the lesson plans, a search for Internet projects is an easy one. Let's try it again, only this time be very specific. Perhaps a search for 5th grade language arts Internet projects.

We've Found the Best Long Distance Plan! 5 cents per min. Long Distance Calling Plan! Save over 40% versus AT&T, MCI and Sprint!

  Get $10 off $100, use code **RINGS** on checkout

Your search for (5th grade language arts Internet projects) found 7 pages of 100 results.

Page 1   More: 1 2 3 4 5 6 7
Results: 1 to 16   Hide Summary · Hide Source · Group Results

1. Mrs. Hodges' Fifth Grade Language Arts ***
Internet Projects & Web Activities, Parents' Place & Parents as Partners. Character Education, "Explore" Resources "Explore" Pacing Guide. 5th Grade Language Arts
http://www.liberty.k12.ga.us/bridge/hodges5th.htm
Source: [Yahoo, MSN, Teoma]   (Translate)

As you can see, Fossick returned 100 hits, with the first one being exactly what we asked for. Did you notice how we didn't need to use Boolean operators?

When joining in on an existing project, remember to ask yourself the following questions: Are you equipped technologically to handle the project? How long does the project last? Is there adequate time for you to integrate it into your classroom activities? Lastly, are you and your students Internet skilled enough to handle the project?

You might also want to visit some of my favorite Internet project Web sites. The first we will visit is Global Schoolhouse located at http://www.gsn.org.

Launched in 1995, this is one of the oldest and most complete repositories for K–12 classroom Internet projects from around the world. It includes a searchable archive based upon age, discipline area, level of expertise, and technology used.

This is also the home of the fantastic mailing list, HILITES. This free list provides teachers with a wealth of classroom Internet projects on a regular basis. It is also a great place to find projects to join or post yours for others to join.

Creating Your Own Classroom Internet Project

There are six steps involved in creating your own Classroom Internet Project. Using these quick and easy steps to layout your project in advance will save you countless hours of rebuilding.

1. Decide what you want your students to learn by doing this project. Keep in mind ways to assess the success of the project as you design it. Outline your goals and expectations.

2. Select one of the three types of projects: Interpersonal Communication, Data Collection, or Problem Solving. Keep in mind that the latter requires much more planning, execution, and data manipulation. Taking "baby steps" is often the best way to introduce a new teaching method, especially when both students and teachers are on the learning curve.

3. Select a topic and name for your project. Make them sound as interesting and exciting as possible. For example, "The Dirtbag Project: A look at soil pollution around the world."

4. Decide the geographical scope of your project. Do you want it to be local or worldwide? How do you intend to announce your project? How many participants do you want?

5. Establish when you want the project to start and how long it will run, with an exact ending date. Be sure to announce a deadline for those wishing to participate, so they have ample time to send in their data.

6. Once the project is complete and your data collated and charted, be sure to share the results with all participants. The best way to achieve this is to have your students create a Web page with the posted project results on your schools Web site. Send an email message to all participants inviting them to visit your school's Web site to see the results.

Beginning a project requires much forethought on the part of the initiating teacher. It is often better to have several teachers in a building collaborate on creating a project than to try one on your own. Start out with an Interpersonal Communication project before you try a problem solving one. It will give you and your students an equal opportunity to gain some valuable experience before launching into a full scale, many-school, worldwide project. Besides, communication is the most important part of doing an Internet project in your classroom.

Use the template worksheet on page 124 to outline and help organize your classroom Internet Project. Feel free to photocopy this page for future use. The following is a brief explanation of each template item.

Project:	Give your project an interesting or exciting name to make others around the world curious. For example, "Are there monsters living under your bed?" Use it to engage your students.
Description:	Provide a brief overview of the project, to whet other's appetites.
Time span:	How long will your project run? Projects over 30 days in duration can sometimes become burdensome if not extremely exciting.
Grade level:	Specify what grade level participants you prefer for your project.
Announcement:	How do you plan to announce your project online? Select a Mailing List and post on your Web site, if you already have one.
Educational goals:	What do you want your students to learn by doing this project?
Geographic/ Demographic areas:	List the geographic and demographic scope of your project; Your school district, the county, state, national, continent, or the world. Do you want only English-speaking participants?
Materials:	List the materials participants will need to complete the project.
Internet Activities:	List those parts of the project that require online time.

Non-'Net Activities: List those parts of the project that are conducted offline.

Final Activity: What specific activities will students need to perform to successfully complete the project? A multimedia or PowerPoint presentation? Write a report? Give an oral presentation in small groups?

Assessment: How will you assess the effectiveness of the project in terms of meeting your educational goals? Creation of computer-generated spreadsheets, charts, graphs? Persuasive essays? Holistic grading? Oral, written, or multimedia presentations?

Internet Project Template

Project Name_____

Description _____
_____
_____
_____

Project time span _____ **Grade Level**_____

Project will be announced via _____
_____

Educational Goals _____
_____
_____

Geographic/Demographic area covered _____
_____

Materials _____
_____

Non-Internet Activities _____
_____
_____

Internet Activities _____
_____
_____

Final Activity _____
_____
_____

Assessment _____
_____

Getting Other Schools to Join Your Project

As mentioned earlier in this section, the best way to get other classrooms to join in on your project is by joining a good Mailing list or two and announcing the project there. When announcing the project, be sure to include the following items:

* Name of the project   * Beginning and ending dates

* Deadline for data submission   * Description of the project

* State the purpose of the project   * Specific subject areas covered

* Grades level(s)   * Number of participants

* How to register, via email, snail mail, etc.?

Note: Be sure that the project falls within your schools curriculum guidelines. Keep your initial project as simple as possible, keeping within the confines of your classroom, county, or state.

For example, create a tour guide for all the historical landmarks in your state. Have classes that reside near an historical landmark, send you electronically the facts, photos, maps, etc. Your class puts together the tour guide.

Announce your project on a Mailing List (s) at least 3–4 weeks prior to its start. Allow participants ample time to prepare for the project.

10 Classroom Internet Project Suggestions

It is sometimes difficult to find the ideal classroom project on the Internet. You know what lesson you want to teach, but just can't come up with an idea for a project. I have included the following list of sample project topics to give you an idea of what other educators around the world are doing to integrate technology into their classrooms.

Project Name: Sometimes They're hot, Sometimes They're Not

Description: This interdisciplinary middle school project revolves around an interactive stock market competition between classmates using real-time stock market data from the New York Stock Exchange and NASDAQ. Students use both traditional and Internet searches to find the necessary information. Each student researches and selects a minimum of four stocks, two from each exchange. They are given $1,000 each in Monopoly™ money to make their purchases. Each student maintains a stock portfolio for one semester. They are assessed at the end of the semester with a required written report describing their results, including graphs, charts, and spreadsheets.

Project Name: Can Poverty be Eliminated?

Description: Designed for middle school social studies students, this project requires them to use both the Internet and traditional resources to research poverty around the world. This project goes beyond the typical campaigns to collect clothes or raise money for the needy. Students use telecommunications (email) to find out how others view poverty, its devastating effects, causes, and possible ways to eliminate it entirely. Students must write a persuasive essay addressing one of the following statements: "If poor people tried harder, they wouldn't be poor." or "If I were in charge of the world, this is how I would eliminate poverty."

Project Name: Special Team Math

Description: Recommended for grades 6–12, this project makes the teaching of basic statistics more interesting and relevant to your students. Students choose their own NFL special team, selecting only a Quarterback, two Running backs, and two wide receivers. They are then required to keep track of each player's statistics for a four-game period. Statistics might include:

Quarterback:	# of passes attempted
	# of completions
	# of interceptions
	# of total yards passing
	# of touchdowns points thrown
Running Backs:	# of carries per game
	# of yards per game
	# of yards per carry
	# of points scored per game
Wide Receivers:	# of receptions per game
	# of yards per game
	# of yards per reception
	# of points scored per game

After the four-game period, students compute the necessary averages for each player on their team, and the team as a whole. They then compare their team's results to the Green Bay Packers for the same four-game period. Students gather data from the NFL's Web site, *USA Today*, and other Internet and non-Internet sources.

Project Name: Are there Aliens in Your Backyard?

Description: Students take a real field trip near their school or home and observe, identify, and record five common plants (corn, milkweed, dandelion) and animals (horses, cows, pigs, dogs) living in their area. Schools from around the world are invited to do the same, emailing their data to the sponsoring school or class.

- One group of students create drawings from half the combined list, pasting their art to a world map showing where the plants and animals live along with a brief description of each.

- A second group simultaneously searches the Internet for descriptions and photographs of the other half of the list. They download images and descriptions, print them out, and paste them on the world map.

- When each group is finished, groups are reversed so that they all have a chance to draw and research them on the Internet.

- All participating students are required to write a short story about their favorite plant and animal from the developed list.

Project Name: Just for the Chill of It

Description: 3rd to 5th grade students from around the world exchange descriptions of their local weather, the kinds of outdoor activities they engage in after school, and the kinds of clothing needed for such pursuits. As messages arrive, many students may be surprised that winter is not the same everywhere. After pinpointing the sources of these messages on a world map, students formulate some relative observations about geography and winter weather. If your timing is right, some students will be sledding while others are riding bikes or swimming.

Project Name: Who am I and Where do I Come From?

Description: Designed for grades 9–12, this multidisciplinary project requires students to research their family's genealogy on the Internet. When completed, they are required to create a family tree and write a narrative of their family's history. They must include maps showing their family's place of origin, as well as a geographical and demographic overview of the area. Students are required to cite the online resources they used, including how the search was conducted.

Project Name: Are There Monsters Under Your Bed?

Description: This fun project is designed to ignite the natural curiosity in students from grades 6 to 9. Classes from around the world are invited to email their local stories or legends about Bigfoot, Sasquatch, or Yeti to the sponsoring school.

They also email a description of the area in which they live, for example, forested, rural, urban, mountainous, etc. Each sighting or story location is then located and marked on a world map. Students are required to search the World Wide Web for such stories and cite the resources they find. The stories are then compiled in a fun book and posted on the sponsoring schools Web site for all participating schools to enjoy. Students learn about legends, myths, and geography as well as how to email and employ proper Internet search techniques.

Project Name: Cloudy with a Chance of Learning

Description: This multidisciplinary project is primarily designed for secondary students. It can, however, be easily restructured for any grade level. Its intent is to help students gain a perspective of how weather affects our lives financially. This cooperative learning exercise requires students to communicate with other peers nationwide in an effort to create a database of temperature, rainfall, and crop grown. Special attention should be given to drought and flooding prone areas using an electronic survey form. Participants complete the survey stating all the above, plus dollar amounts of annual crop damage caused by the forces of nature between 1994 and 1996. Students then search the Internet for data from the stated time periods for price fluctuations of crops grown in those areas. Students are required to develop charts, graphs, and spreadsheets demonstrating those price fluctuations and to plot the regions of severe, moderate, and least affected areas of the country. Students write a position paper outlining their ideas of how the government can better deal with price fluctuations caused by abnormal weather.

Project Name: Garbage, Yuk!

Description: This 6th grade project requires students to develop a survey form that outlines recycling programs in schools around the country. This data collection project helps students identify better methods of dealing with the growing problem of waste management in this country. Students are required to post the survey on two mailing lists and create a collated list of ideas into a database. Working in teams of three or four, they search the Internet for information about the amount of garbage generated by the major cities across America. They contact experts in the field of waste management via email from the "Ask an Expert" site on the World Wide Web. Based on their research, they draw conclusions in writing about how their school rates in terms of recycling compared to the rest of the country. They also compose a written report discussing how they would personally deal with this growing problem, and then give an oral presentation to the rest of the class. The presentation should include downloaded images of garbage dumps or other graphic representations of how severe the problem is becoming. The results of the project are placed on the schools Web site to share with the other participating schools.

Project Name: 'Net-opoly

Description: This fun project can be designed for any grade level or discipline area(s). Students create a game board much like Parker Brothers' *Monopoly*™. They create each space on the board as a Web site containing certain questions about each day's lesson. Each Web site is assigned a value from 1 to 300 Megahertz, depending on the difficulty of the question. Students work in teams of three or four. When a team successfully locates the Web site, prints out the information, and properly cites the resource, they place their team's name over that square. If they fail to find the correct resource, they must spend the next day in the "Virtual Principal's Office" (jail).

Students create draw cards for clues to locating the resources and spaces on the board with "School Library" and "Guidance Office" upon which they must land to receive a clue card. Eventually, all the Web sites will be claimed. The team that has accumulated the most Megahertz wins. This project generates a lot of excitement in the classroom.

Sharing Your Internet Project Results

Even if your completed classroom Internet project is done only within the confines of your classroom, you should still consider the value of sharing the results with the educational community. Educators are constantly mining the Internet in search of the perfect KeyPals or projects for their classes, sometimes ending up frustrated after constantly coming up empty. As more and more classrooms venture into computer-aided instruction, more and more information and teacher resources will become available. We must continue to share that information with our colleagues if we expect them to do the same with us.

The main reason the Internet works as well as it does is because people like you are willing to invest time and energy into sharing your online and offline experiences. If your project has required the input of others from next door or around the world, you have a responsibility to share the results, especially if you ever want them to participate in future projects.

Your students also benefit greatly from the experience of helping create your school's Web pages. Use Web page construction as an educational opportunity. Kids are curious by nature, and introducing them to the world of HTML will only continue to spark their curiosity. Most educators recognize the importance of problem solving, critical thinking, and using higher-order thinking skills. Web page creation facilitates all of these.

Back in the good old days, the traditional instructional model of read, listen, and practice worked well for learning lower level facts or skills. However, today's teachers are more attuned to the fact that they must actively engage students in the process of their own learning. Maybe we should offer a new degree for teachers called "Edutainment."

Research is beginning to show that the use of technology and computers in the classroom is aiding in the educational process. Children in the world learn at their own rate and with their own style, and computers can accommodate those differences. Computers are patient and can therefore provide the constant feedback ADD or ADHD students require. It only makes sense that we focus more on active learning when integrating the use of technology into our classrooms. Providing a student with the opportunity to offer input into their instructional model lends itself to the development of better self-esteem. As we all know, good self-esteem is the secret to success in school and later on in life, in general. Helping students become consciously competent should be one of our main goals in school today.

Summary

An Internet project can be anything you want it to be. It can be short, long, simple, complicated, or difficult. What matters the most is that students get a feel for the way education is changing, that they begin to see the importance of technology in their lives, and develop a better appreciation for it. Classroom projects are not necessarily going to create more or less work for educators, they are simply new and different methods to present much of the same information.

Recent studies show that certain changes occur when computers are introduced into the classroom. We are noticing a difference in patterns of interaction, classroom organization, and student learning. Throughout the projects listed here, I continually stress the point of students working in small groups. Studies are showing that students who work in pairs or groups of three or four, develop peer interaction as a form of classroom participation. Students are beginning to help one another through the learning process and becoming better equipped to deal with classroom conflicts resulting from a variation in views.

The success of computers in the classroom is directly tied to a teacher's willingness to embrace this new technology. It is the way in which teachers present and use new methods or materials that most greatly impact the success or failure of new approaches to learning. The skill and knowledge of a teacher using a given tool or method has the largest positive impact on student learning. Computers are here; we must now find the best ways to use them in our classrooms.

Online Internet Project Web Sites

I have listed a few of my favorite Web sites containing educational resources, Internet projects, KeyPals, and more. Merely conducting a search for **Internet Projects** will turn up a fantastic wealth of projects done by teachers for teachers. Adding your specific discipline area after **Internet Projects** will narrow your search considerably.

KeyPals.com
http://www.keypals.com/p/keypals.html

KET Internet Projects
http://www.ket.org/Education/IN/projects.html

Education Place
http://www.eduplace.com/projects/

Kids@work
http://www.globalclassroom.org/projects.html

Global Schoolhouse
http://www.gsn.org

I.E.C.C.
http://www.iecc.org

A Special Thank You

The Internet project ideas used in this section come in part from the many seminars and in-services I have conducted over the past 10 years with educators from around the world. These educators have realized that technology such as the Internet is becoming an integral part of their classroom instructional model. They diligently completed their in-class requirements by helping to create these fun, yet educational learning experiences for their students. These 100,000+ educators are far too numerous to list here; however, I thank and commend them all for a job well done.

One last project Web site you may wish to visit is:

The Creative Connections Project

http://www.ccph.com/

Connect your class to a class in the Amazon rain forest, Africa, China, the Arctic, or the Galapagos. A must-visit Web site for all K–12 teachers. Recently selected as a Teachers Featured Site at TonyBrewer.com.

Section 12 — WebQuests in the Classroom

What is a WebQuest?

A technology-based WebQuest, as defined by its developer, Dr. Bernie Dodge of San Diego State University, is a structured learning activity that requires students to conduct the bulk of their research and information gathering on the World Wide Web.

WebQuests are, by nature, a fun and exciting new element being added to classroom presentations all over the world. Using WebQuests, teachers are able to engage and perhaps re-engage students.

WebQuests are not only fun and exciting for nearly all students, but are also proving to be a reenergizer for teachers. Tired of presenting the same old lessons in the same old manner, teachers everywhere are desperate for a change. Technology is providing the perfect vehicle to cure their boredom.

Components of a WebQuest

One of the special and unique features of a WebQuest is the ease of development. The following breakdown of the integral components will help you in designing and presenting your WebQuests.

Introduction

The Introduction is written with the student as the intended reader. Given that understanding, you can create an Introduction that is fun, exciting, and draws your students in. In the Introduction, you write a short paragraph to introduce the activity or lesson to the students. If there is a specific scenario involved here is where you'll set the stage. Remember that the purpose of this section is to both introduce the activity and hook the reader. The Introduction is also where you address the premise upon which the WebQuest is built. On the following page is an example of an excellent Introduction paragraph from an award-winning WebQuest created by Amy Trumpeter, a teacher at Fuller Middle School in Framingham, MA.

Here is a look at this WebQuest's Introduction. Notice how it draws students into the activities and spurs them to learn more.

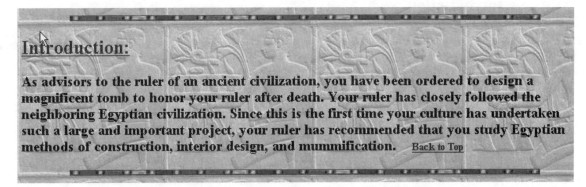

Introduction:

As advisors to the ruler of an ancient civilization, you have been ordered to design a magnificent tomb to honor your ruler after death. Your ruler has closely followed the neighboring Egyptian civilization. Since this is the first time your culture has undertaken such a large and important project, your ruler has recommended that you study Egyptian methods of construction, interior design, and mummification.   Back to Top

Tasks

Describe crisply and clearly what the end result of the learners' activities will be. The task could be a:

- problem or mystery to be solved;
- position to be formulated and defended;
- product to be designed;
- complexity to be analyzed;
- personal insight to be articulated;
- summary to be created;
- persuasive message or journalistic account to be crafted; or
- a creative work.

The Task:

1. Divide your group of advisors into three teams to become experts in the following areas:

    A. Architecture and Engineering
    B. Preparation of Bodies (Mummification)
    C. Tomb Preparation (Including Religion, Hieroglyphics, Interior design, etc.)

2. Investigate your assigned area.

3. Prepare and present your team's plan to your ruler in the form of a PowerPoint presentation.

In this particular WebQuest, the creator has divided the class (Advisors) into teams, with a clear, concise set of tasks, assignments, and outcomes.

If the final product involves using some tool (e.g., HyperStudio, the Web, video), mention it here. Don't list the steps that students go through to arrive at the end point. That belongs in the Process section.

Process

To accomplish the task, what steps should the learners go through? Describing what is expected in the Process section helps other teachers see how your lesson flows, and how they might adapt it for their own use. Remember that this whole document is addressed to the student. Below are a couple of Process statements:

1. First, you will be assigned to a team of three students.

2. Once on a team, you will decide what role you wish to play

Notice how well this teacher has detailed the Process section.

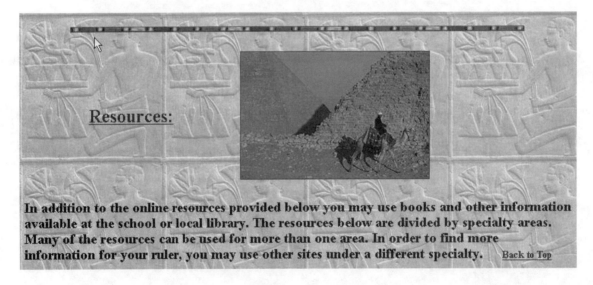

The Process:

1. As a team of advisors, investigate your assigned area using the Internet resources provided below and other outside resources to gather facts regarding Egyptian methods related to your specialty.
2. Share your findings with other members of your group.
3. Schedule formal or informal meetings with your ruler to share your progress and seek guidance.
4. Prepare a group presentation using PowerPoint for your ruler.
5. Be sure to use rubrics provided throughout research.
   REMEMBER: Support your plans with facts from your Egyptian research.
6. Present your final plan to the Royal Court.
7. Ask questions and seek advice if you need help.
8. HAVE FUN!!!!!   Back to Top

Learners access the online resources that you've identified as they go through the Process. You may or may not have a set of links that everyone looks at as a way of developing background information.

If you break learners into groups, embed the links that each group looks at within the description of that stage of the process. Your resources belong in the Process section.

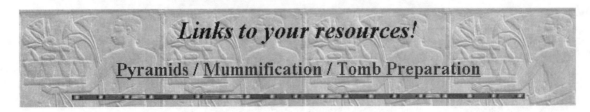

Resources:

In addition to the online resources provided below you may use books and other information available at the school or local library. The resources below are divided by specialty areas. Many of the resources can be used for more than one area. In order to find more information for your ruler, you may use other sites under a different specialty.   Back to Top

This teacher embedded the Resources as hyperlinks in the Process section.

Links to your resources!

Pyramids / Mummification / Tomb Preparation

In the Process block, you might also provide some guidance in how to organize the information gathered. This advice could include suggestions for using flowcharts, summary tables, concept maps, or other organizing structures. The advice could also take the form of a checklist of questions to analyze the information, or things to notice or think about. If you have identified or prepared guide documents on the Web that cover specific skills needed for this lesson (e.g., how to brainstorm, how to prepare to interview an expert), link them to this section.

Conclusion

Write a couple of sentences here summarizing what they will accomplish or learn by completing this activity or lesson. You might also include some rhetorical questions or additional links to encourage them to extend their thinking into other content beyond this lesson.

Notice how this WebQuest clearly states what the expected outcomes are.

Conclusion:

Through this Webquest you will travel back in time to the lands of Ancient Egypt. You will have the opportunity to be immersed in the culture and daily life of the Egyptians. This journey will improve your understanding of Ancient Egypt. You will become a great resource for your ruler in the areas of pyramids, mummification, religion, hieroglyphics, tomb preparation and much more! The research you will conduct will help your ruler prepare for the afterlife. I hope that you will enjoy your journey and have a safe flight on your travels home.

Assessment

Describe to the learners how their performance will be evaluated. Specify whether there will be a common grade for group work vs. individual grades.

Notice that this WebQuest specifies that evaluation will be team-based.

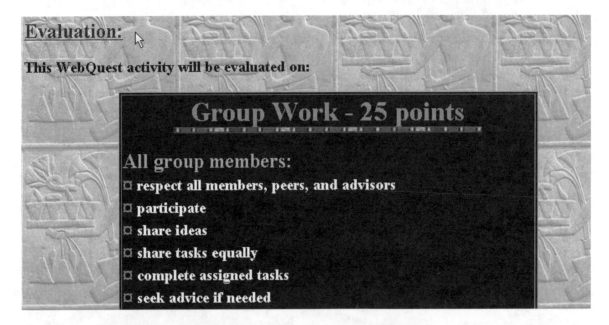

This WebQuest also places the bulk of the evaluation on the final product, a clear, concise PowerPoint presentation.

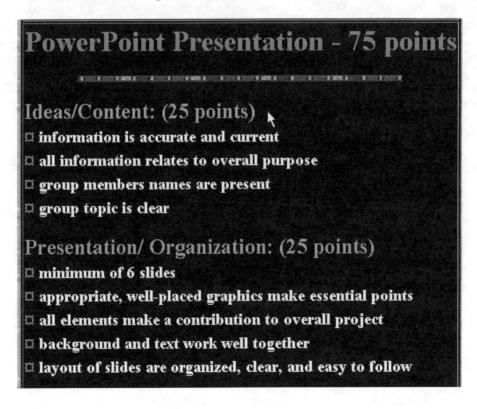

Language and Mechanics: (25 points)
- organizational structure is clear
- grammar, punctuation, and spelling is accurate
- is thoroughly proofread and without careless errors

You will want to create a scoring rubric for your particular WebQuest. I suggest that you visit Dr. Bernie Dodge's Original WebQuest page at: http://webquest.sdsu.edu/

Credits & References
List here the sources of any images, music, or text that you're using. Provide links back to the original source. Acknowledge anyone who provided resources or help. List any books and other analog media that you used as information sources as well.

WebQuest Development Resources
The following list of WebQuest online resources have been culled from the thousands available. Each has been carefully reviewed and determined to be an excellent resource for helping you design a student-inspiring WebQuest.

Spartenburg Webquests
http://www.spa3.k12.sc.us/WebQuests.html

EdHelper
http://www.edhelper.com

EduHound
http://www.eduhound.com

Education World
http://education-world.com

The following WebQuests have been selected from the thousands available online because of their unique qualities and effective use of technology as an instructional tool.

Art and Music
http://www.spa3.k12.sc.us/WebQuests/Impressionism.htm

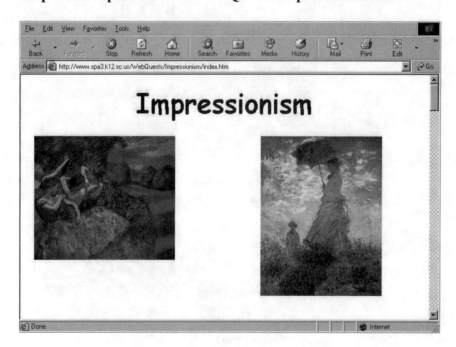

http://www.berksiu.k12.pa.us/webquest/Ballein/index.htm

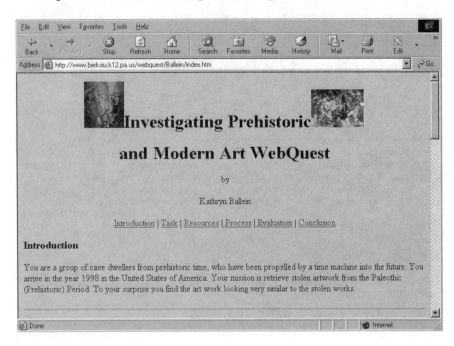

Business Education

http://warrensburg.k12.mo.us/webquest/entre/index.htm

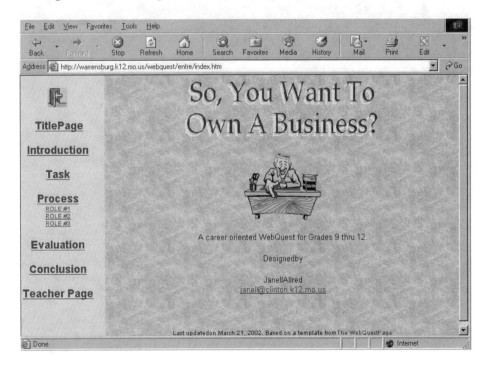

http://www.plainfield.k12.in.us/hschool/webq1/webquest.htm

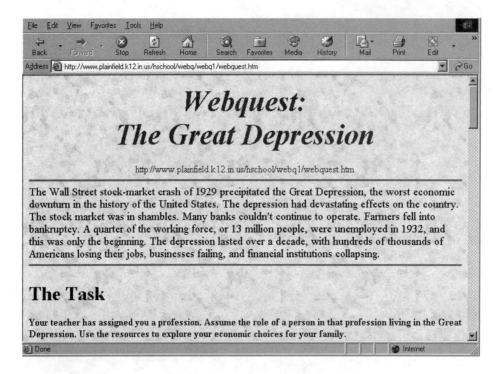

History

http://www.itdc.sbcss.k12.ca.us/curriculum/civilwar.html

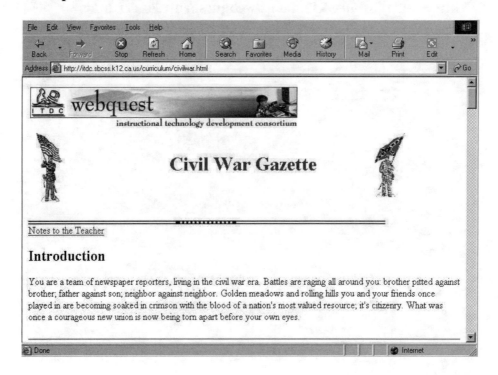

http://www.kn.pacbell.com/wired/BHM/tuskegee_quest.html

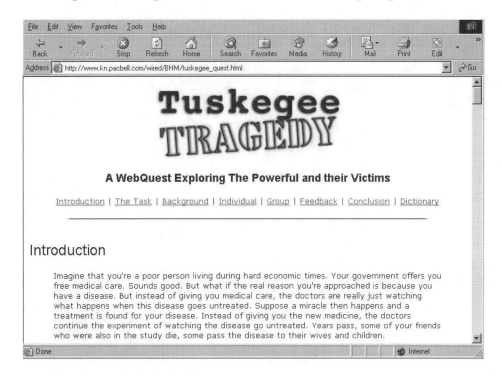

Native Americans

http://www.berksiu.k12.pa.us/webquest/historyss.htm

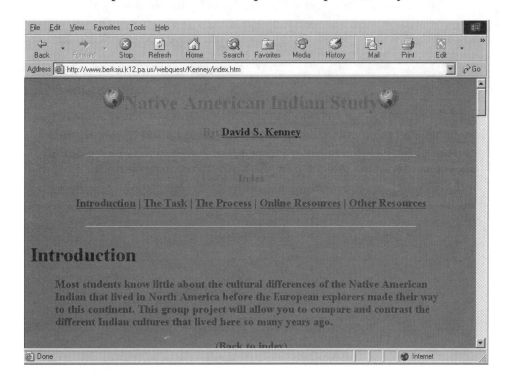

http://www.memphis-schools.k12.tn.us/ admin/tlapages/web_que.htm

http://www.itdc.sbcss.k12.ca.us/curriculum/oldones.html

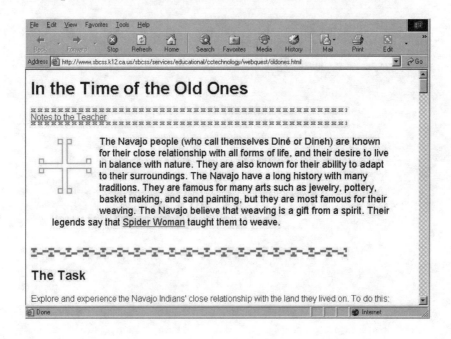

Foreign Language

http://www.teach-nology.com/teachers/lesson_plans/computing/web_quests/social_studies/

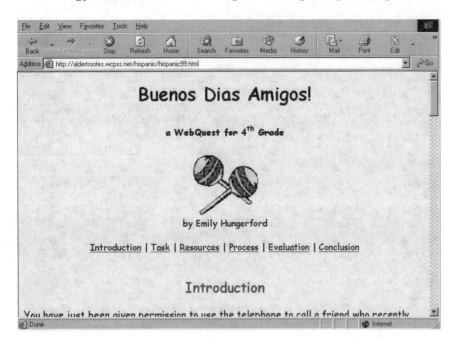

Social Studies

http://www.kn.pacbell.com/wired/democracy/debtquest.html

http://coe.west.asu.edu/students/ccallaway

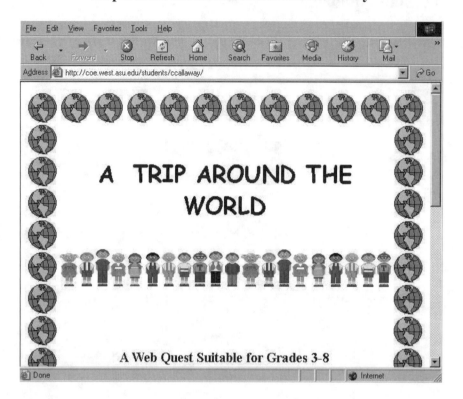

Writing

http://www.berksiu.k12.pa.us/webquest/astheimer/default.htm

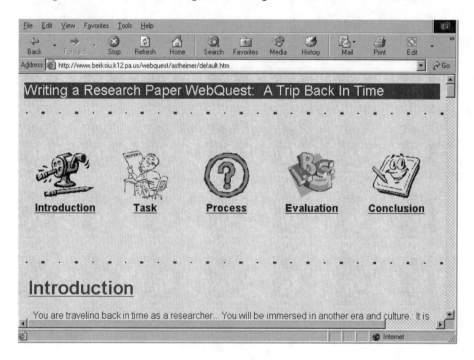

http://www.itech.fcps.net/trt10/Webquests/writeon.htm

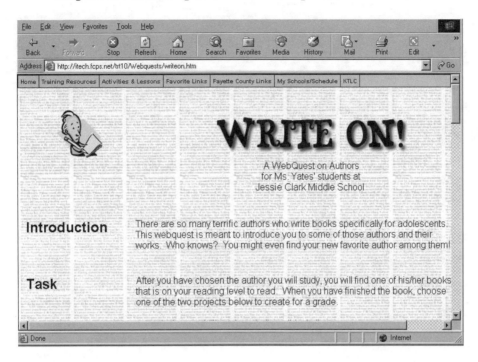

Math

http://www.bellmore-merrick.k12.ny.us/webquest/math/mag.html

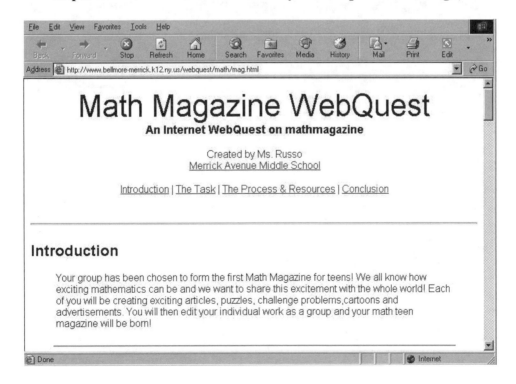

http://www.sinc.sunysb.edu/Stu/rgonsalv/mathwebquest.html

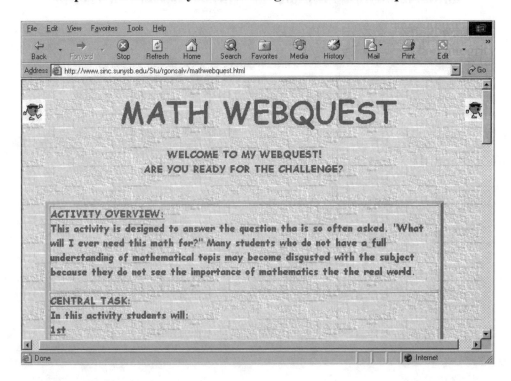

Science

http://warrensburg.k12.mo.us/webquest/penguins/

http://www.memphis-schools.k12.tn.us/admin/tlapages/butterflies.html

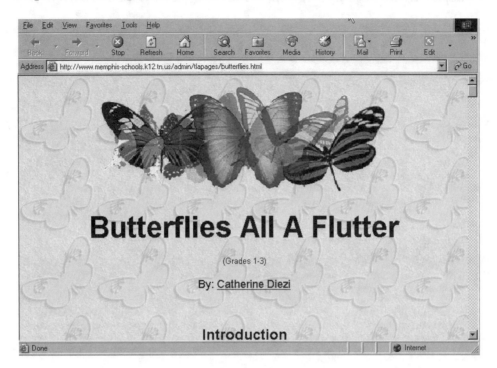

http://www.davidson.k12.nc.us/webquests/endanger/endstart/endstart.htm

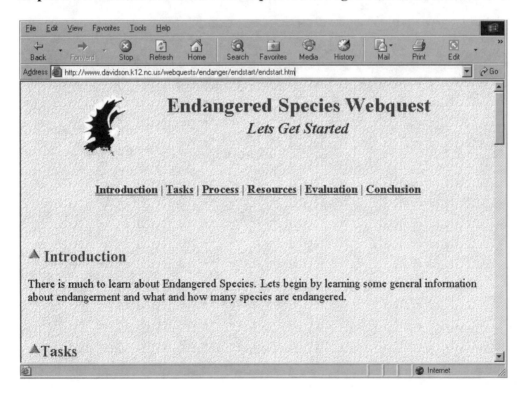

http://ourworld.compuserve.com/homepages/RayLec/acidrain.htm

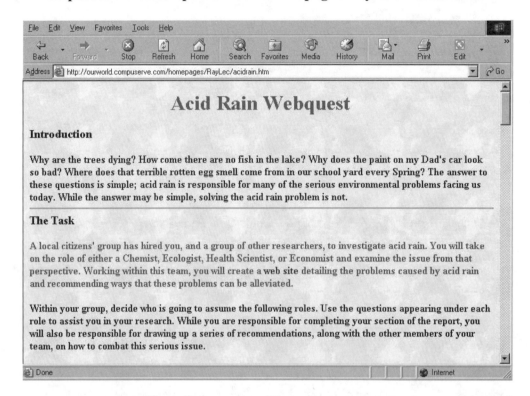

http://www.memphis-schools.k12.tn.us/schools/ ibwells.aca/biomes.html

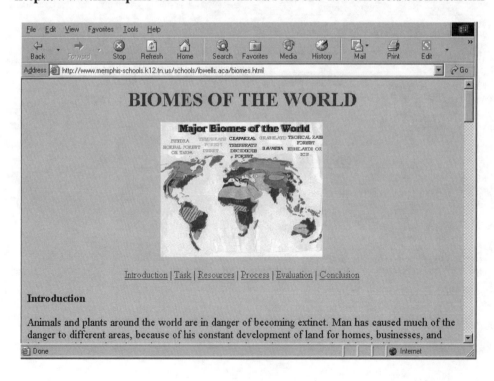

http://cte.jhu.edu/techacademy/fellows/ Hammond/WebQuest/kkhindex.html

http://btc.montana.edu/ceres/html/mountainquest.htm

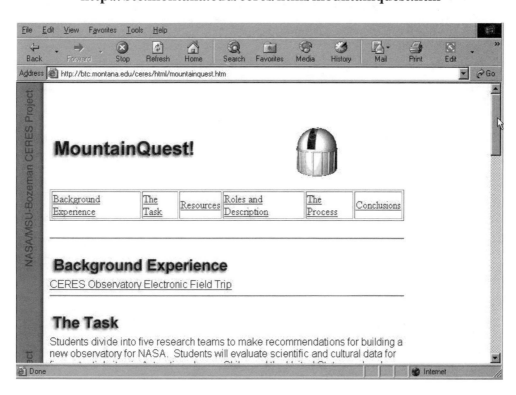

http://www.ced.appstate.edu/whs/goals2000/projects/98/karen/webdinosaurs1.htm

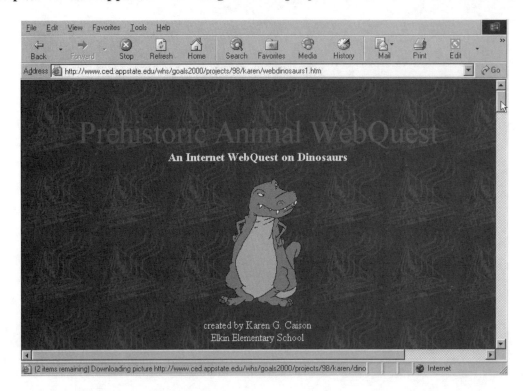

http://aliceswebpage.homestead.com/everestwebquest1.html

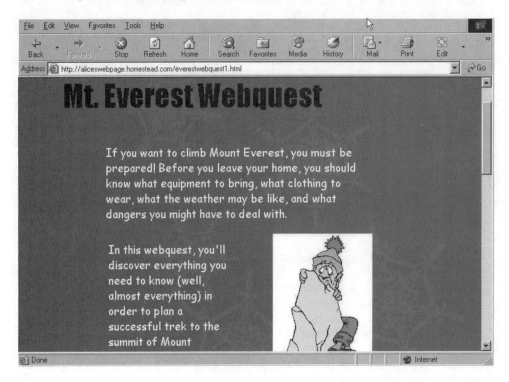

http://webpages.charter.net/gkoprivica/Atlantis.html

http://web.mala.bc.ca/webquests3/bigfoot/index.htm

http://www.biopoint.com/WebQuests/webquest2.html

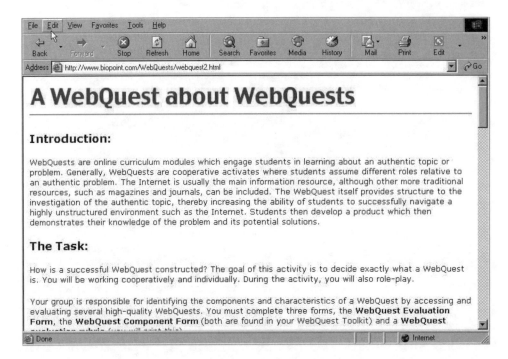

This might be the first WebQuest you do. It clearly covers every aspect of what a WebQuest should be, how it works, and expected outcomes.

Section 13 — The One-Computer Classroom

Introduction

With the many tips and resources in this section, you will discover how having limited computer resources can actually contribute to the effective management of your classroom and help your students learn.

Managing the One-Computer Classroom

Change is inevitable, especially in today's K–12 classrooms. The largest changes have been in the area of technology. Classrooms are abuzz with the sounds of computers humming and keyboards clacking. But what can you do when you only have one or a few computers in your classroom? It's easy to assume that limited computer resources are restricted in their usefulness. Many teaches believe that they will spend all their time helping students use the computer, or that there is no way students can work in teams around one little computer screen. Still others worry if students don't have a lot of individual access to the computer, it can not act as a significant teaching tool in the classroom.

Fortunately, there are many ways to make use of limited computer resources—having limited resources can even be an advantage. A classroom full of computers is more difficult to manage and requires lots of supervision and forethought. Students gathered around one computer can work together, ask each other questions, share ideas, and lead each other through the assignment.

A limited number of computers also permit you to put varying student ability levels to work. Using the team approach, you can link up more experienced students with less knowledgeable ones. When students have trouble, they can ask the more experienced students in their team before going to you for help. To make the most use of your limited computer resources, I suggest three basic approaches:

- Selected classroom activities, such as conducting presentations for the entire class.
- Student collaborative work, such as using the computer as a learning station, or creating a collaborative spreadsheet.
- Independent work, such as having students create Web pages, perform research, or improve typing skills.

Selected Teacher Activities

Having only one or a few computers in the classroom allows you to closely manage your computer resources. The simplest form of managing computer resources is to sit at the computer yourself, either conducting presentations for the class, or completing some of your own work such as grades and lesson plans.

Whole-Class Presentations

There is no doubt that limited computer resources does restrict the amount of time your students are able to spend on the computer. That's why one of the most effective uses of limited computer resources is to lead a whole-class presentation. Your students can participate in using computer technology and learn about new computer software and hardware without the need for individual access to the computer.

One effective presentation involves demonstrating specific hardware or software to your class. For instance, you might find it useful to conduct a whole-class presentation on using Microsoft Word, in which you teach your students the basics about fonts, tabs, bullets, numbering, and other word-processing essentials. It offers your students a head start when using Microsoft Word to write an essay or research paper. Whole-class presentations are also useful in demonstrating computer-related projects that students work on in the classroom or in the computer lab. Perhaps you would like your students to create a PowerPoint presentation about animals that live in the rain forest. You can first show the entire class a sample presentation and explain the different kinds of slides your students can create and the types of multimedia and information you would like to see.

Because your students are not using the computer themselves, there is always the danger that they may lose interest halfway through your presentation. Using multimedia is a great way to enhance whole-class presentations and keep your students engaged. Multimedia can range from PowerPoint presentations with moving text and animated graphics to video that stream over the Internet. A number of radio stations, both in the U.S. and abroad Web-cast their programs. Many special events and conference presentations are also delivered live over the Web in streaming format, so this is a technology that continues to grow and become more and more useful in the classroom.

You can use Internet simulations to take advantage of multimedia over the Internet. Simulations are multimedia-based Internet sites that demonstrate information and activities, such as what happens when two liquids are mixed together or how a car engine works. They provide a packaged, dynamic, and interactive whole-class presentation for your students.

For example, take a look at http://www.modelscience.com.

You might also try out http://www.motionsoftware.com for some examples of simulations.

With any whole-class presentation you conduct, it is important that each student has a clear view of the demonstration screen. In general, teachers should use a television monitor, LCD panel, or video projection system during whole-class demonstrations—without some type of large display, only students sitting directly in front of the computer screen will be able to see. If a large viewing screen is not available, have your students rotate through the demonstration while others are working at independent group activities.

Try book-marking your Web sites so that you can seamlessly run through your lesson. To ensure that technical problems or Internet connectivity issues do not get in the way of your presentation, save a copy of a Web page onto your computer's hard drive. Take a look at our Tutorial for information about saving Web pages at http://www.tonybrewer.com/webwhacking.

If you would like to present streaming audio or video over the Internet, remember that the quality of the media depends on the speed of your Internet connection. It is best to have a high-speed connection such as cable modem, DSL, or a T1 or T3 line. When you are using streaming video in a whole-class setting, you will want to project the image so that the entire class can see it. However, enlarging the video when you project it often produces a blurry image. As an alternative, download the file to the computer's hard drive and have students watch the video in small groups.

Fortunately, playing multimedia over the Internet is a nearly problem-free process these days. To ensure that multimedia plays as seamlessly as possible, make sure you have all the commonly used multimedia tools called **plug-ins.**

The Web site below is one of the best places to locate the classroom enhancing use of multimedia. Netscape and Internet Explorer each have some plug-ins designed for each respective browser. However, most of the ones you will be using work very well on both browsers. If you run across a Web site activity that requires a specific plug-in, the site will tell you what plug-in you need and how to download it.

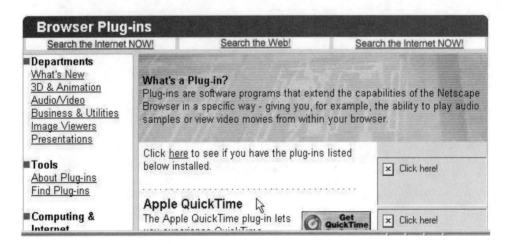

Once you have completed the demonstration, be sure to provide supporting reference material at the computer station, usually in the form of printed step-by-step, illustrated instructions. Pre-searching the Internet for appropriate sites—especially in the earlier grade levels—and creating bookmarks for your students' future use saves time and helps filter out inappropriate material.

It is important to remember that you can actually use the computer to do your own classroom work. The computer provides a much faster, easier, and more accurate way of organizing and maintaining files. With the appropriate hardware and software, you will not only complete your work in less time, but continually sharpen your technology skills as well. Activities and descriptions are tabled on the next page.

Teacher Activity	Description
Recording student grades	Create a read-only file that allows students to view their current grades. Either create the file in an Excel or AppleWorks spreadsheet, or use commercial gradebook software programs such as Thinkwave, Gradekeeper, or 1st Class Gradebook.
Taking attendance	With today's rapid influx of technology, most schools have or are in the process of converting most administrative tasks to the computer, including taking attendance. If your school does not have a dedicated attendance-taking software program in place, you can create a spreadsheet or select from commercially available programs such as Thinkwave or SkyPac.
Classroom inventory control and budget development	Each year, teachers must develop a budget and a list of resources. Keeping a running inventory of supplies you use throughout the course of the school year helps you quickly develop your budget for the following year. The easiest way to develop your budget is to create a simple spreadsheet listing the items you want. You can add the cost of the items to the following year's budget, including the product or service, the suggested suppliers, and the cost.
Develop lessons	Creating new or modifying previously used lesson plans each year can be an incredible chore. But if you store those lessons on the computer, modifying and reusing them becomes a quick and simple task. The computer also allows you to create and save student handouts, worksheets, and assignment and homework lists. In addition, the Internet contains thousands of ready-to-use lesson plans covering every topic imaginable. Using a search engine (such as http://www.google.com), you can quickly find valuable ideas, tools, and information on the Web.
Create and maintain a classroom Web site	With so many students accessing the Web from home, a classroom Web site is a great way to keep your students informed and engaged. Your Web site might include a list of homework assignments, information for parents, or even links to your students' Web projects.
Email parents	In the past, teachers spent countless hours each month mailing or sending home notes with their students to keep parents informed about classroom or school activities. Email allows you to contact parents with a just few clicks of the mouse. You can even use your email program to set up an electronic mailing list that sends one email to all the parents in your classroom. But remember, parents without Internet access will still need to be contacted through notes sent through students or via regular mail.

Collaborative Projects

Whole-class presentations are a great way to make the most of a classroom with only one or a few computers. But how else can you use limited computer resources effectively in the classroom? Because students are not able to spend much time working on computers individually, have your students work on collaborative projects so that they use the computer in teams.

Creating Student Teams

Most teachers and technology training experts recommend that students work in teams ranging from two to four members, especially because the space around the computer usually limits the number of chairs that allow team members to view the monitor comfortably. It is often better to create teams with students of mixed ability levels. If one student has difficulty, other more knowledgeable team members can help out. Each team member should assume the responsibility for a specific part of a research assignment, and students should rotate their roles regularly. Most teachers assign the following roles:

- A recorder, who records the group's work on the **assignment worksheet** and writes down any relevant notes.
- A keyboarder, who operates the computer.
- An idea creator, who offers tips on searching techniques and keywords.
- A technician, who handles any hardware or software glitches.

Learning Stations

One of the best ways to set up collaborative projects is to design the project using learning stations. Learning stations are separate workstations that can range from computers to library research, in which student teams work on computer-related assignments. With learning stations, students get an opportunity to use the computer while making use of other school and classroom resources. To set up learning stations, divide your classroom into different types of learning activity centers. Learning stations might include a:

- traditional resource center, including text and reference books
- computer center
- teacher-directed center
- team discussion and planning center
- multimedia center

In general, four or five learning stations work best for completing assignments and maintaining good classroom control. If you have a significantly larger class size, you might increase the number of learning stations or increase the number of students per team. Try to avoid more than five students per team—students become less engaged if they have too little to do as a team member.

Once you are ready to assign your students to their learning stations, you should:

- Explain to students, in detail, the purpose of each learning station.
- Perform a demo of each learning station before sending students off to their stations.
- Be sure to use Bookmarks/Favorites on the computer.
- List specific Web links for online resources.
- Supply an **assignment worksheet** to keep students on task and supply you with information for tracking their progress.
- Post **computer use rules** for teams that finish early.

With so many teams working independently, it is important to define the amount of time students spend at each station to help manage their progress. The type of project you assign your students and your classroom and school schedules help you decide on a reasonable time limit. Try to keep the amount of time at each station at or below 20 minutes, which gives you time for a lesson introduction and a wrap-up session. The 20-minute limit also helps keep your students from getting bored and restless.

Be sure that your students are aware of how much time they have to work at each station. You can include information about time limits and other guidelines in a list of **computer use rules** that you distribute to your students.

Whole-class Spreadsheets

Students can also work together to create a collaborative spreadsheet, which allows students to research and analyze statistical data. A spreadsheet, consisting of a grid of columns and rows, is the computer equivalent of a paper ledger sheet. Spreadsheets can make calculations simple and easy—all the numbers are instantly recalculated whenever you change any of the variables. With spreadsheets, students can see the progression of calculations on the screen as they are generated and change one variable at a time to see what effect the change has on the overall calculations. Students can even generate charts so that they have a visual representation of the trends they are analyzing. Because spreadsheets are based upon numbers and calculations, they work best with projects that involve tracking data over a period of time, such as the yearly rainfall in Brazil or the temperature changes during the month of April.

When using collaborative spreadsheets, it is important to assign students to specific roles:

- Data collectors (those who collect the data)
- Data-entry specialists, (those who enter the data)
- Data checkers (those who verify that the data has been entered correctly)
- Designers (those who contribute to the design of the spreadsheets)

Make sure to monitor your students' progress to ensure that their data is reliable and that they are on task.

Independent Student Work

Limited computer resources make it challenging for students to have individual access to the computer or computers in your classroom. But there are still times when students will have some time to work on the computer individually. You have several options available for students that work independently on the computer.

Ask an Expert

Although computer work is often considered a solitary task, the whole-class demonstrations and collaborative projects offer demonstrated ways of making computer work a shared, interactive experience. Even when students work independently on the computer, the Web is overflowing with hundreds of subject-specific experts that are happy to electronically communicate with your students and answer their questions.

Ask an Expert is a list of online, accessible experts in almost every topic imaginable, from the Amish and Astronomy to Rodeo Journalism. You can find **Ask an Expert** at http://www.askanexpert.com. With Ask an Expert, students can use experts as a resource for their individual projects. Teachers can point students to Ask an Expert for questions they can not answer or for topics that require specialized knowledge. In the lower grades, teachers can use Ask an Expert to complement lessons that teach communication and technology skills. One possible drawback to asking a question of an online expert is the response time. In many cases, responses occur within hours, but sometimes, depending on the expert's schedule, a day or two may pass before your students get a response. It is important that your students are prepared in case the expert takes a few days to respond.

Try having your students develop a set of potential questions at the start of the project so that they can contact the expert as early in the project as possible.

Developing a Class Presentation

Demonstrating a multimedia presentation for the class allows students to take their individual computer skills and share their work with others, exercise their creativity, and develop their public speaking skills. PowerPoint and HyperStudio are the most popular software programs used for presenting information in a dynamic slideshow format. Text, charts, graphs, sound effects, and video are just some of the elements that students can incorporate into their presentations. To keep slideshows running smoothly, give students guidelines for sizing fonts, charts, and graphs so that their presentation can be seen from the back of the room. It is best to use a television monitor, LCD panel, or video projection system to enlarge the image. Be sure that your students do a run-through on their own to check for errors or problems before they present their work to the class.

Independent Workstation

One computer contains many tools and provides access to vast amounts of information via the Internet. To take full advantage of these tools and resources, your classroom computer can function as an independent workstation that students can reserve to work on their own projects. We have provided three workstation suggestions as a starting point.

Research workstation	Students can search the Web for almost any kind of information, including looking up words, mapping locations of streets, parks, and buildings, and reading about important historical trends and events. Be sure to bookmark some good search sites such as http://www.google.com or http://www.fossick.com to help get them started.
Multimedia workstation	Using PowerPoint, Photoshop, Dreamweaver, or any number of graphics, audio, or Web tools, students can work at creating Web pages, computer-based art, or even composing their own electronic music.
Typing workstation	Independent computer time is a great opportunity for students to enhance their typing skills. *Mavis Beacon Teaches Typing*, *Nimblefingers*, and *Magictype* are just a few of the typing programs available.

When you set up the computer as an independent workstation, create a sign-up sheet so that students know when the computer is available and can reserve a block of time on the computer.

Special Challenges in the One Computer Classroom

As with any specialized learning tool, computers in the classroom present their own unique series of challenges and headaches.

Students with Different Amounts of Computer Experience

There can be a wide array of computer knowledge and experience in your classroom. That is why it is important to assess your students' computer skills and knowledge using **technology knowledge pre-assessment** before giving them access to computer resources. A pre-assessment allow you to quickly discover the amount of support each student requires, as well as assisting you in pairing students according to their skills and computer knowledge.

Once you have an idea of your students' ability levels, you can take several steps to accommodate for their needs:

- Hold small demonstrations for the less experienced students while the rest of the class works at learning centers.
- Give less knowledgeable students independent tasks on the computer to help them build their skills.

- Pre-plan your teaching assistant's time to work with the less knowledgeable students.

You can also assign different roles to your students based on their knowledge level. The more knowledgeable students can be "technical advisors" that you pair with students needing help with software problems, Internet questions, or computer assignments. Technical advisors can also work independently, researching and pre-book-marking sites for future lessons.

Accommodating Students without a Home Computer

Some students may lack computer experience because they are without a computer at home.

You can assist these students in several ways:

- Provide supervised after-school access to computer labs and the school library.
- Create a school/public library association, in which students can have evening and weekend access to computers.
- Develop homework assignments that can be done digitally or manually.
- Set up a donate-a-computer program with local businesses.
- Contact computer companies that offer schools special lease packages—they usually average around $50 a month per computer.

Dealing with Computer Problems

A sudden and mysterious computer crash or software glitch can spoil the best-laid plans for delivering curriculum with a computer. Using your technology knowledge pre-assessment, you can select a group of students to become members of a **peer swat team** who help out when your computer starts acting up.

Try assigning one or two specialties to each member of the team according to their skills and knowledge. Your peer swat team can help you with problems ranging from hardware issues and printing problems to working with multimedia, using specific software programs, and saving files. Make sure the swat team members understand that they should only become involved with computer problems at your request.

It is also useful to develop a **troubleshooting checklist** that addresses the most common technical issues. Do not hesitate to contact your building's technology specialists or coordinator if your peer swat team and troubleshooting checklist cannot solve your problem.

When computer problems occur while students are working on collaborative projects, you can give students a list of steps to follow before they ask you for help. Make sure students:

- Try to solve the problem among the members of their learning station team.
- Go through the Troubleshooting Checklist.
- Consult the "Help" tab found on most software programs.

- Request the help of the peer swat team.
- Ask the teaching assistant (if one is available).

Working When the Internet is Unavailable

Unfortunately, your peer swat team and troubleshooting checklist are unlikely to help during the inevitable periods when the Internet is unavailable. The best option is to save Web sites to your hard drive so that they are accessible even when the Internet is down. Before your whole-class demonstration, you can save the Web sites you will be using so that those Web pages are available whether or not you have access to the Internet.

There are two options for saving Web pages:

- Try a step-by-step guide to saving a Web site using Internet Explorer in Section 8.
- Use WebWhacker™ software. More information on WebWhacker can be found at http://www.bluesquirrel.com

If you would prefer not to save Web pages to your hard drive, try printing out the Web pages before your demonstration. Conduct the lesson using the printed pages if the Internet goes down.

Arranging Multiple Computers

If you have more than one computer in the classroom, you must decide how to arrange them. The most important rule is that all computer monitors should face toward the center of the room—never toward the walls—so you can monitor what students are doing at a glance. To get you started, I have provided models for several different room layouts.

One Computer

In a one-computer classroom, the computer should be placed at the front of the room so the teacher can perform live demonstrations using an overhead or video projector or TV monitor.

Several Computers

In the several-computer classroom, all computers should face toward the center of the room, never towards the walls. Several suggested room layouts are featured on the following page.

Layout 1

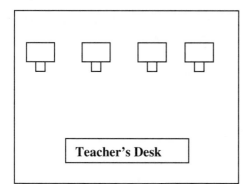

Layout 2

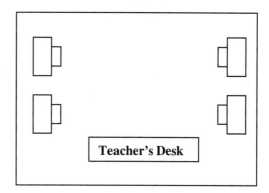

Layout 3

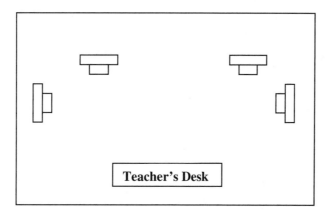

The most critical issue is to have the computer monitors visible to the teacher at all times. This aids considerably in monitoring students' online activities. Are they accessing inappropriate material? Are they actively engaged in their online project or activity? Are they having any difficulties?

Because printers are noisy and can become a distraction when multiple groups are waiting for their printouts, try placing the printer in the corner farthest from your learning stations. If multiple groups are printing at the same time, some print jobs will be delayed while others are printing. Make sure your students understand that their pages will print and that they should only press the print key once. You might want to assign one of your peer swat team members to monitor the printing activity.

Computer Management in the Lab

The lab provides a chance for students with limited computer access in the classroom to work individually on their technology skills. Because each student has access to a computer, the lab is especially useful for allowing students to work on more sophisticated software that requires a lot of independent work and study. Students can also work on skills that they can only improve through independent work, such as typing.

Pre-planning for the Lab

When planning your students' work in the lab, it is essential to begin with a solid lesson plan that allows your students to work independently. To make the best use of the limited amount of lab time you have, prepare your students for the work they will be doing. Discuss with your students exactly what will be expected of them, including assignments and behavior, before you go to the lab.

Make sure you consider the amount of time your students will have in the lab as you create your assignments. It is best to either create a project that is short enough for students to finish by the end of their lab session is or to make sure students get several blocks of time in the lab within a fairly short period. Try saving Web pages to the computer's hard drive or book-marking so that your students can make the most of their lab time. Also be sure to provide your students with an assignments checklist to keep them on task.

Although computer labs provide an opportunity for each student to have individual access to a computer, younger students often work better in groups of two or three to a computer. They usually share the responsibilities of the assignment and support each other when difficulties arise. As students advance through the grades, the need for self-directed access becomes more important.

Practicing with More Sophisticated Software

When students are trying to learn a sophisticated software program such as Photoshop, it is essential that they have a solid chunk of time to independently exercise their skills and investigate the different options and tasks they can perform. To give them a head start before they go to the lab, conduct a whole-class presentation in the classroom that demonstrates the basics of the software.

An entire class of students working independently on a sophisticated software program is bound to keep you on your toes with questions. To help manage your students, develop and distribute a list of frequently asked questions (FAQs) that they can refer to at their individual computer stations. If they cannot find an answer using the FAQ, have students ask your computer swat team. You might also be able to minimize the questions if you anticipate and answer them in a whole-class presentation conducted right before you go to the lab.

Using Software that Requires Individual Access

While a classroom with unlimited computer resources offers a wide array of opportunities for students to practice their technology skills, they will probably not be able to work on skills that require a lot of individual access, such as typing. The lab is a great opportunity for your students to practice those skills.

It is best to have all your students working on the same skill so that they can help each other out when questions or problems arise. Make sure that you and your computer swat team is ready to help those students who are progressing a little more slowly and might require some guidance.

Dealing with Computer Problems

As with your classroom, your peer swat team and troubleshooting checklist should be your first defense against computer problems that crop up in the lab. It is probably best to discuss technical problems with the lab teacher first, if one is available, because the lab teacher may be familiar with your particular technical problems already.

It is also important to account for network problems, which prevent your students from accessing files stored on the server. Remind your students to save their work often, and have them save their work to a folder on the desktop so they can work on it whether or not the network is available.

Technical issues are not the only problems that arise in the lab. What should you do when there are a few computers in the lab that are more powerful and sophisticated than the other computers? It makes little sense to place students on computers they do not know how to use. At the same time, every student should learn to use all of the available computers and software programs, which are often only available on the "good" computers. To solve this dilemma, set up the more sophisticated computers as peer tutor sites. The more skilled students can work with those that are less knowledgeable, which improves the self-esteem of the peer tutor while helping students that need guidance.

If you are looking for other ways to handle a computer lab of students with differing amounts of computer knowledge and experience, have your students complete a technology knowledge pre-assessment. Younger students (K–4) usually work best in pairs, so your pre-assessment will help you join students whose abilities and knowledge complement each other. Older students can work more independently. Use the pre-assessment to prepare for the students that are most likely to require help. The pre-assessment can even help you pre-plan the services of your teaching assistant or lab teacher, should either be available.

Additional Resources for the One-Computer Classroom

Search Engines
http://www.google.com

http://www.fossick.com
http://www.mamma.com
http://www.vivisimo.com

Web Whacking
http://www.bluesquirel.com

One-Computer Classrooms
http://mariposa.scdsb.on.ca/sservices/infot/onecomputer.htm

Hotlist
http://www.kn.pacbell.com/wired/fil/pages/listonecompja.html

EduHound
http://www.eduhound.com/cat.cfm?subj=One%20Classroom

Typing Programs
http://www.crackinguniversity2000.it/DmozComp/index-2689.htm

One-Computer Classroom Management

Simulations
http://www.scotese.com/pangeanim.htm

Scavenger Hunts
http://www.spa3.k12.sc.us/Scavenger.html

Additional Resources for the One-Computer Classroom

Virtual Reality Tours
http://www.pbs.org/nova/pyramid
Ask an Expert
http://www.askanexpert.com
Interacting with other students:
http://www.epals.com
Grade software comparison
http://www.education-world.com

Projects for the Computer Lab and Classroom

http://www.gsn.org
http://www.iecc.org
http://www.sofweb.vic.edu.au/gc/projects.htm
http://www.ket.org/IN/projects.html
http://www.eduplace.com/projects
http://www.onlineclass.com

Examples of Online Demonstrations

Simulations
http://www.scotese.com/pangeanim.htm

Scavenger Hunts
http://www.spa3.k12.sc.us/Scavenger.html

Virtual Reality Tours
http://www.pbs.org/nova/pyramid

Glossary

Bookmark: A shortcut to a previously viewed Web site. Create and access bookmarks though a Web browser such as Internet Explorer, in which they are called "Favorites."

Higher Order Thinking Skills (HOTS): A program dedicated to improving a student's problem solving, data analysis, and language arts skills.

Learning station: A separate workstation, ranging from computers to library research, where student teams work on computer-related assignments.

Network: A group of computers in a small area that can communicate directly with other devices in the network, such as the server.

Server: A hard drive on a different computer that is used to store files and folders. The server is accessible by any computer in the classroom or lab.

Web browser: A software application that allows you to view the World Wide Web. The most common Web browsers are Internet Explorer and Netscape.

Web Whacking: Downloading an entire Web site or set of Web pages onto a local machine, so that you can access them again without reconnecting to the Web.

You should be all set to begin using your computer more effectively in your classroom. It can be a powerful tool that engages students and teachers in the learning process.

Section 14 — Copyright, Plagiarism & the Internet

Plagiarism

What do we call it when a student uses the Internet to search for and locate information, then copy and paste it into a word processor? Plagiarism—unless they cite their resources and paraphrase their writings' contents. While it is certainly true that the Internet has been one of the greatest inventions of modern time, it can also be a source of consternation for educators. Prior to the Internet's development, students relied upon textbooks, school libraries, and other forms of print media to gather information for essays, term papers, and other teacher-assigned writing tasks. Verifying a student's work was relatively easy.

Today, access to a seemingly endless fund of information is right at a student's fingertips. Whether researching a term paper on a specific aspect of the American Civil War or writing a critical essay on the situation in the Middle East, students need only log-on, look-up, and download. The opportunity for assignment completion without the use of critical thinking skills is far too often so tempting that even the trustworthiest of students have difficulty demonstrating proper ethical behavior. The old axiom that *character is how we act when we're alone* has never been truer.

Unethical student copyright violations have indeed become an international epidemic. Cheating has become prolific in every elementary, middle, and high school around the world. The statistics on cheating are absolutely alarming. While surveys on K–12 student cheating run the statistical spectrum, the vast majority of surveys demonstrate an ever-increasing problem. Here are a few of those challenging statistics.

According to the Gallup Organization, the top two problems facing the country today are: 1) Education; and 2) Decline in Ethics (both were ranked over crime, poverty, drugs, taxes, guns, environment, and racism, to name a few) (Gallup Organization, October 6-9, 2000)

The following are some statistics from *STUDENT CHEATING AND PLAGIARISM IN THE INTERNET ERA: A Wake-Up Call* (Libraries Unlimited, June, 2000)

- 80% of high school students admit to cheating on a test
- 67% of high school students say they have copied someone else's homework
- 98% of K–12 students say they have let others copy their work
- 90% of high school students who cheated avoided getting caught
- 34% of all students said their parents never discussed cheating

Even in elementary schools, cheating has become so common that in a recent writing contest in Atlanta, three of the 10 finalists were disqualified for plagiarizing. (Gary Rathgeber, Superintendent Canon Elementary School District)

Cheating on tests, homework, term papers, and essays has become a high-tech habit and kids are using everything from voice and text pagers, email, and especially the World Wide Web to deceive their teachers. Teachers and parents must form a strong line of communication to combat this pervasive assault on our educational system. In addition, our system must make a concerned effort to provide both with the tools necessary to monitor student copyright, attribution, and plagiarism issues. Ethics is more than merely cheating on tests; it is a violation of human trust and student integrity.

Plagiarism.org is an outstanding Web site that every K–12 teacher, parent, and student must visit. All three groups can gain a better understanding of the latest information on online plagiarism and what tools are now being used by educators, all over the world, to fight plagiarism and help return academic integrity to our schools. This site will also open the eyes of naysayers who refuse to realize the breadth and depth of the most serious problem to infest the hallways and classrooms of our educational institutions. You will want to spend some time here.

The site is filled with nearly all the information you will need to make informed decisions, regarding the cheating plague. If we, as a society, are to properly prepare today's students for tomorrow's workplace, we must undertake a comprehensive K–12 program of re-education in the areas of personal integrity, critical thinking, skills development, and respect for other's intellectual property. The handwriting is on the screen. We must provide educators with the appropriate tools to reverse this disturbing trend.

The first of these tools can be found on the **Plagiarism.org** web site and is called **Turnitin.com**. Touted as the world's leading plagiarism prevention system, the following map beautifully illustrates the levels of digital plagiarism on a state-by-state basis.

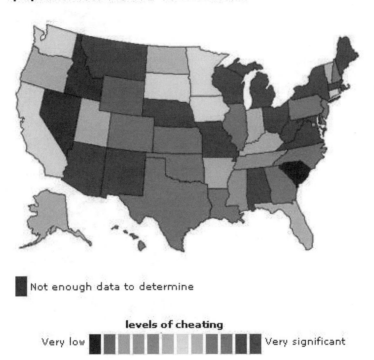

Notice the preponderance of yellow, gold, orange, and red colored states. It gives one pause to consider the ramifications of such a widespread problem. Unfortunately, not all parents feel that plagiarizing online resources is an infraction of school policy that justifies punishment. Here is a prime example:

Earlier this year a school board in Kansas fell to parental pressure by overturning a teacher's decision to fail students who had plagiarized research papers. Columnist Tucker Carlson (*Reader's Digest*, July, 2002) suggests that the newest right to be wrung out of the Constitution will be the right to cheat.

Students function better and are more comfortable when they are required to work within certain educational boundaries. Ethics must be a part of that plan.

As mentioned earlier, teachers and parents must have tools at their disposal to help combat the trend towards cheating as an alternative to learning. Many students actually believe that plagiarism is acceptable...as long as you don't get caught! That statement alone indicates that students know that plagiarism is wrong.

Below is a look at one of the best plagiarism prevention programs I have come across at **Turnitin.com**.

Unfortunately, this is not a free program, but its extremely low cost of approximately 50 cents per student per year makes it well worth the investment. The online aspects of this service and speed of information recovery also make it a pleasure to use.

Here's how **Turnitin.com** works:

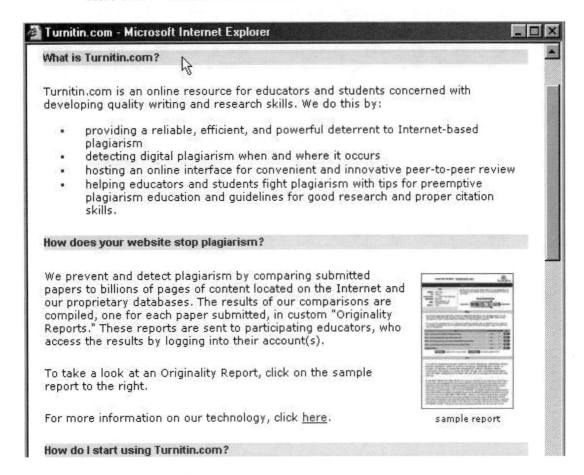

You must register for this service and submit a request for a quote for your particular school.

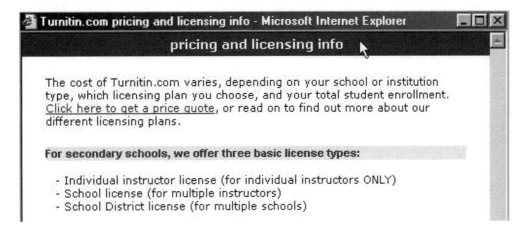

Everyone agrees that gaining the ability to read and write are the foundations upon which all learning is based. When young students begin to learn to write, they mimic what they see, copying down letters of the alphabet exactly as they see them. As they progress from letters to short sentences, and then to more complex sentences, they again copy them exactly as they see them. Those are examples of expected plagiarism.

As young learners blossom into competent readers and writers, they are expected to continually develop critical thinking skills. It is when that process allows them to reach a reasonable level of competence that we expect them to begin recognizing the importance of citing other people's work. We can not expect the young mind to innately understand the need to recognize other's work. But, we must instill within them the reasons to do so.

Perhaps the best method to instill the need for citing other people's work is through the use of real-life examples. Here is a potential real-life scenario question:

Do you think it is fair to pay people to listen to music they created? If you answered yes...What if you created a new song that became very popular, would you like it if someone else copied it and made all the money from it instead of you?

Perhaps the following list can be used as a basis for helping young students gain a better understanding of the need for crediting other people's work.

- Use real-world examples to demonstrate the personal aspects of copyright, plagiarism, and attribution.
- Have your students create their own list of reasons to properly cite both online and offline resources.
- Make sure a copy of the rules for citation and evaluating online and offline resources is at every computer station.
- Use early infractions as an example of what not to do, not necessarily to punish. Be forgiving early and gradually tighten the requirements.
- Students seem to adhere more closely to classroom rules when engaged in collaborative learning exercises. Use this type of activity whenever possible.
- Reinforce the efforts that students demonstrate, even though they may not be totally correct. Use these incidences as learning opportunities.
- Work on character-building skills daily.
- Use online and offline books, stories, or anecdotes to demonstrate good character, honesty, and virtue.

Perhaps the following lesson plan developed by the Center for the Advancement of Ethics and Character can properly illustrate the point.

An Elementary Lesson Plan

The Empty Pot:
A lesson about integrity
The Empty Pot (Demi, 1990) can be used to discuss the importance of integrity

Summary: Demi's tale is set in ancient china. The wise emperor is growing old and must choose a replacement for his crown. The flower-loving ruler devises a task for the children of China and announces that the most successful participant will be made his successor. Each child is given a seed to see who can grow the most beautiful flower.

Young Ping, who is an outstanding gardener, has little doubt he will grow a great flower for the emperor. However, despite his great care and attention, Ping's seed will not grow. When the day finally arrives and the emperor orders all of the children to bring their flowers to be inspected, Ping is saddened to see so many children rushing by with their beautiful flowers. Ping is ashamed. He has nothing to show. He approaches his father for advice. His father tells him that his pot, although lacking a beautiful flower is sufficient; He had done his best, and he must tell the truth. So young Ping goes to the village with his empty pot.

The emperor looks sadly at the beautiful flowers before him. At last he approaches Ping. He asks Ping why his pot is empty. Ping explains that he did his best to grow the flower but it just would not grow.

The emperor smiles and exclaims that he has found his replacement. He reveals that all of the seeds he had given to the children were COOKED and therefore could not grow. The test was not to find the greatest gardener, but a child with the integrity needed to rule wisely in China.

Awareness
Discuss the maxim "honesty is the best policy" with the class. Have the students ever heard this phrase before? What does it mean to them?

Understanding
Read *The Empty Pot* to the class, stopping at different intervals in the narrative to ask the following questions:
- What did Ping think about the contest to grow the most beautiful flower at the beginning of the story?
- Did Ping try his best to help the seed grow? How do you know?
- What does Ping think of his friend's suggestion to take another flower to the emperor? What do you think he should do?
- Do you think Ping's father gave him good advice?
- Why do you think the emperor seems unhappy with all the beautiful plants?
- What had the emperor done? Why?
- Do you think Ping was the best choice for emperor? Why?
- What do we mean when we say Ping showed integrity?
- What is integrity? In what ways did Ping show integrity?

Action
- Ask students to make posters illustrating moments in time when Ping showed integrity.
- Challenge students to create a class "integrity" pledge. This pledge should be posted in the classroom and referred to throughout the year.
- Help students create a bibliography of books that remind them to act with integrity.

Reflection
- Ask students to evaluate the importance of sharing a story like *The Empty Pot* with other children their age. Would they recommend that other teachers or parents read this story to second graders? Why?
- Ask students to consider whether or not they would want a friend to have integrity. How would they know if a friend had integrity?

This lesson is an excellent example of how easy it is to demonstrate a point regarding integrity. I'm sure you can locate through searching the Web for even more lesson plans and classroom activities that do the same.

While good grades that reflect learning, not the ability to cheat, is most desirable, we need to focus heavily on the desired outcomes from the following list.

Expected Student Outcomes

- Develop good self-esteem as a product of responsible behavior.
- Assume responsibility for their actions.
- Know "right" from "wrong."
- Respect the rights of others.
- Work cooperatively with others.
- Develop decision-making and problem-solving skills.
- Use self-discipline to achieve goals.
- Resist negative peer pressure.

Copyright

In a nutshell, a copyright gives the creator the right to:

- reproduce the work
- permit copies to be made by others
- prepare derivative works
- display the copyrighted work publicly

Copyright begins the instant someone creates something. Whether it is a sketch a of new building, a cartoon, a musical piece, or a Web site, it belongs to the one who created it for life, plus 70 years if it was created after 1978. Nearly everything created since 1923 is still copyrighted.

How about Fair Use Rules for Schools?
Generally speaking, Fair Use Rules in schools can generally be covered by addressing the four areas listed below:

- What is the purpose of copying?
- What type of work are you copying?
- What is the number of copies you intend to make…8,000 copies?
- What is the effect of use…students learn?

To become more knowledgeable on the subject, I recommend a visit to http://www.starvingartistslaw.com/industries/educators.htm. This site is dedicated to helping teachers, students, and parents become better acquainted with copyright laws.

So, the bottom line is quite simple for students, whether copying and pasting from:

- Web sites
- CDs
- Networks
- Email messages
- Photographs
- Audio or Video files
- Traditional resources

The message is always the same...*Cite it*!

Term Papers of the 21st Century = Multimedia Presentations

Multimedia Presentations (2003 guidelines)

- Use material as created
- Use limited amounts
- Use citations
- Use for direct instruction
- Use in class, but
- Students may keep for portfolios
- Teachers may keep for parent conferences

Software
- Read the fine print

Borrowing from Web

- Audio/video files
- Graphics
- Content
- Check for trademarks (™) as well

Always check for Trademarks before borrowing images, logos, etc. without permission.

Set Policies and Procedures

- Make them clear
- Explain, then use examples
- Model the policies and procedures
- Enforce them

"To cite or not to site, that is the question." (Shakespeare…sort of!)

- When in doubt, ask for permission
- Cite all sources, no matter what.
- Cite Web pages, including date viewed

Use either MLA or ALA Style citing
http://www.ala.org…..American Librarians Assn.
http://www.mla.org….Modern language Assn.

Checking Up on Students
Look for clues in student work that indicate it is not their work. You may even use:

- Anti-plagiarism software programs
- Glatt Plagiarism Program (http://www.Plagiarism.com)
- Plagiarism.org (http://www.Plagiarism.org)

Check Term Paper Mills Online
- A1-Termpaper (http://www.a1-termpaper.com/)
- Evil House of Cheat (http://www.cheathouse.com/uk/index.html)
- Research Assistance (http://www.research-assistance.com/)
- Term Papers on File (http://www.termpapers-on-file.com/)

Other Alternatives

Give Creative Assignments

- Specific topics (not generalities)
- Use a rubric (Designing a Rubric. San Mateo County Office of Education. http://pblmm.k12.ca.us/PBLGuide/Activities/DesignRubric.html
- Conduct a WebQuest (See Section 11)
- Add non-written elements that require synthesis or verbal explanation.
- Include comparison or reflective activities

Have students use their own creative designs or consider the following:

- Create your own graphics
- Use copyright-free graphics
- Animation Factory (http://www.animfactory.com)
- To Whack or not to whack, that is the question
- Blue Squirrel (http://www.bluesquirrel.com/storefront/storefront.html)
- Awesome Clip Art - Free Clip Art
- Free Stuff Center (http://www.freestuffcenter.com/clipart/index.html)

Some helpful sites to visit regarding Copyright, Plagiarism & Attribution

Sharon Williams. Avoiding Plagiarism. Hamilton College. October 1, 1999. http://www.hamilton.edu/academics/resource/wc/AvoidingPlagiarism.html

American Psychological Association. Electronic Reference Formats. October 1, 1999. http://www.apa.org/journals/webref.html

Groton Public Schools. Copyright Implementation Manual. October 1, 1999. http://groton.k12.ct.us/mts/egtoc.htm

Bedford St. Martins. Rules of Citation. Dec. 2002 http://www.bedfordstmartins.com/online/citex.html

New Life Beyond Yahoo. Dec. 2002. http://servercc.oakton.edu/~wittman/find/copyrite.htm

Copyright and Plagiarism Quiz http://smccd.net/accounts/karas/english/copyquiz.html

When and if all else fails, be sure to visit the "Mother" of all libraries,
The Library of Congress at: http://www.loc.gov

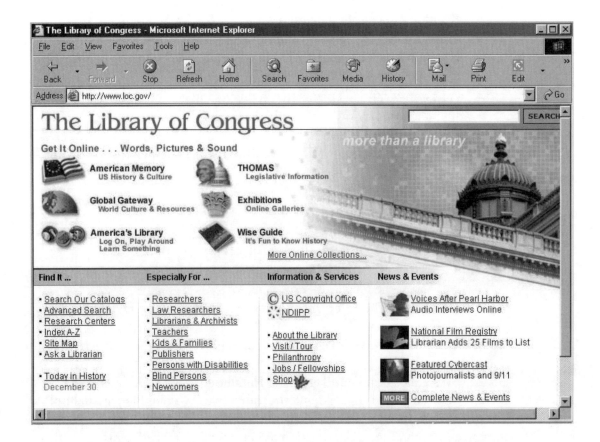

Section 15 — Student Assessment & Electronic Portfolios

Assessing Student Performance in the 21st Century Classroom

There appears to be a direct connection between being rated or evaluated for performance and the level of performance for which an individual strives. The problem with this type of standardization is how it may result in greater loss of positive self-esteem, as it inevitably leads to those who win and those who lose.

Authentic assessment strategies build on the real life experiences and abilities of students, not standardization. Authentic assessment is ongoing and is placed more directly in the hands of students, encouraging more personal responsibility. This type of assessment is collaborative; involving peers, teachers, and especially, parents. Authentic assessment focuses on an individual's strengths, abilities, experiences, and multiple intelligences. For more information on multiple intelligences, I highly recommend Walter Mckenzie's new book.

Multiple Intelligences and Instructional Technology: A Manual for Every Mind. Eugene, Oregon: ISTE, 2002. ISBN 1-56484-192-8.

Authentic assessment is used for the improvement of learning. It is focused on successful learning, not simply improving performance assessment.

Creating Electronic Student Portfolios

Portfolios are intended to be accurate reflections of a student's individual and group progress, and play an increasingly important role in authentic assessments. The inclusion of student artifacts and teacher observations in the portfolio help ensure greater student engagement, and are more reflective of an individual student's achievement in real-life situations versus the traditional methods of assessment.

Portfolios provide a wealth of feedback to students, teachers, parents, higher education institutions, and possibly future employers. In that light, we must ensure that a student's portfolio is representative of their skills across the media spectrum.

The transition from traditional assessment portfolios to an electronic format has been a natural progression. Ease of access and distribution enables a closer integration of assessment processes with instructional goals, learning styles, and teaching practices.

An electronic portfolio is a deliberate digital collection of student artifacts that illustrate a student's personal creativity and progressive achievement. The key is that students select the bulk of their portfolio's content, with significant teacher input.

Unlike standardized tests, electronic portfolios are direct indicators of a student's real-life learning experiences. Portfolios lend themselves greatly to the overall understanding of a student's cognitive and emotional growth, and are especially useful during parent/teacher conferences. Teachers can share with parents' portfolio content that is a much truer indicator of a student's growth and performance.

Electronic portfolios are also perfect vehicles for interaction during student/teacher conferences, often including a student's real-life learning experiences and future direction as they relate to curriculum. It is very important to continually maintain student portfolios to draw comparisons of student growth. Today's classroom-enhancing technology makes electronic portfolios the primary ingredient in the recipe for successful learning.

Today's classroom teachers are beginning to regard electronic portfolios as an excellent opportunity for alternative, authentic assessment. This decision is very good news. Unfortunately, teachers everywhere are struggling with how to get started. The following is a series of suggestions to help you get started.

Vision
Teachers need to develop a clear vision of what they want to include in an electronic portfolio, and how to go about collecting the artifacts. Teachers should consult local, state, and national standards to ensure that the areas of assessment are within the proper guidelines.

Assessment Methods
Once a teacher has chosen the parameters for artifact inclusion in the electronic portfolio, they must determine what assessment method to use. Perhaps the best way to do so is by creating specific categories such as: **artifacts**, **process**, and **reflections**.

Artifacts are actual student work. They may include writing samples, multimedia presentations, artwork, or any other physical work they create.

Process is evidence of a student's involvement in the assessment strategy. Process might include rough drafts of essays or term papers, stated goals, and objectives.

Reflections play an important role in the assessment strategy for individual students. We need to have them reflect upon their work in a realistic, non-judgmental way, determining their own level of involvement, motivation, and self-assessments of their learning. We often find that students are much tougher on themselves than we are. It is, therefore, extremely important that we help temper the degree to which they complete the self-assessments, supporting them in their areas of strength rather than weakness.

Collaborate on Portfolio Content

The use of electronic portfolios makes it possible for students to easily review their own work. We must allow students a lions-share of the judgment in determining what actually goes into their portfolios. It is, however, very important for teachers to offer supportive input on what artifacts to include.

Students need frequent access to their portfolios, especially if we want to provide them with enough time to thoughtfully reflect upon their work. Another interesting exercise is to have students collaborate by reviewing each other's portfolios in a supportive, realistic manner.

Choosing What to Include in an Electronic Portfolio

Unlike parents who keep every little scrap of refrigerator art their child creates, teachers and students need to be a little more discerning in choosing what to include in a portfolio. While the initial reaction might be to include only the best examples of student work, the reality is to provide the portfolio viewer with a wide array of student work, showing progress wherever it occurs.

This is especially true in the area of product development, wherein the journey is often more important and educational than the end result. We need to be sure to include any artifacts that demonstrate the students continual, improving grasp of the process, as the student works along the project time continuum. As each project is completed, students need to reflect upon the process, their individual involvement, and level of motivation.

Organizing the Electronic Portfolio

Electronic portfolios should be organized in a manner that demonstrates a clear and accurate picture of the student's growth, performance, and motivation. It should be organized so that teachers, students, and parents are able to easily identify specific assignments and tasks while observing the student's level of involvement, motivation, and growth.

Generally speaking, a portfolio should include a:

- clear, concise table of contents
- description of each task or project
- time-stamp of the event
- student reflection on the task, assignment, or project
- authentic assessment rubric used to assess student performance

Electronic portfolios are only as good as a teacher's determination to use them. Teachers must be willing to dedicate the necessary amount of time and energy to ensure an effective result. Former First Lady and current State Senator

Hilary Rodham Clinton stated that *"it tales a village to educate a child."* In this case; however, it takes a teacher's and a school's willingness to move away from standardized models of assessment and take that leap across the digital divide.

To gain a better understanding of what a good electronic portfolio looks like, I have included the following examples graciously provided by Tammy Worcester, Instructional Technology Specialist, ESSDACK.

Card 1 — Title Card: The title card features a picture of the student. The picture could be scanned from a printed photograph or taken with a digital camera.

Clicking on the picture activates a button that plays an audio recording of the student.

Card 2 — Table of Contents: This card serves as a link to all other cards. The viewer can click on an invisible button over each "folder" to go to that page.

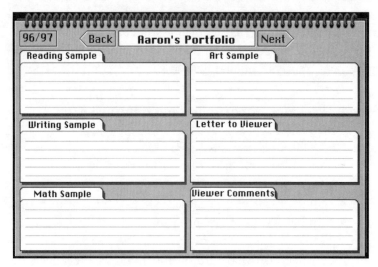

If desired, the student could write a reflection of the activity in the space below the title on each folder.

Cards 3–6 — Work Samples: The right side of the "book" shows an excerpt from a book. When you click the button at the left, it activates an audio recording of the student reading the section.

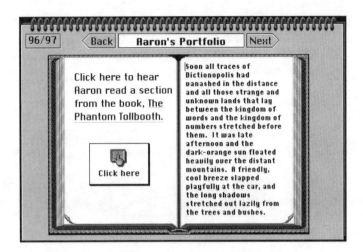

Card 5 contains a letter from the student to the viewers. **Card 6** shows comments the viewers write to the student.

Developing Assessment Rubrics

Traditional methods of student assessment are quickly being replaced by 21st century methods. As discussed earlier in this section, more emphasis is being placed on student-centered learning, with assessment strategies being modified to compliment the shift.

One of the many advantages technology provides is the use of online rubric generators. There are several very good Web sites that provide more than 50 assessment rubric alternatives. The next few pages contain several sites for you to peruse.

Type http://www.teach-nology.com into your browser's address box. Once loaded, select the **Rubrics** link from the top menu as shown below.

Teach-nology is an excellent Web site, providing not only an outstanding array of assessment rubric generators, but also downloadable worksheets, lesson plans, and some excellent teaching tips.

The screen capture below shows a few of the rubric possibilities. I've selected the *Project Rubric Generator.*

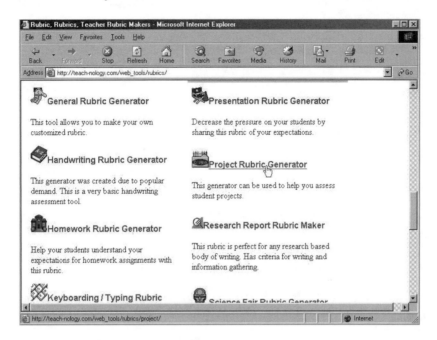

The rubric generator begins with the selection of an image to identify the rubric.

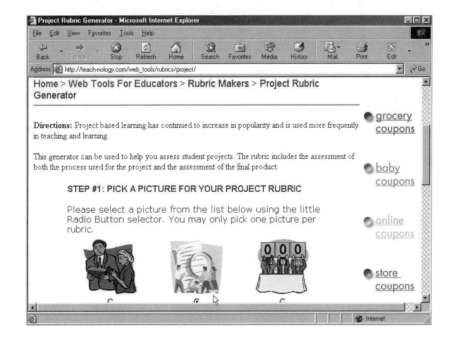

Select an image and scroll to the bottom of the screen, shown on the next page.

Fill in the information requested in the form below.

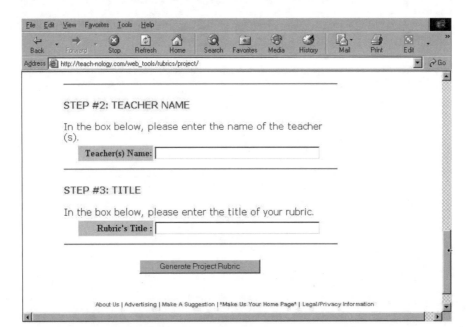

Click on **Generate Project Rubric** and your new rubric will appear as shown below.

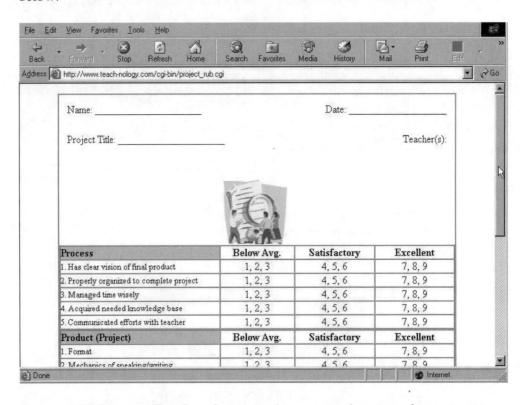

As you will discover, **Teach-nology.com** has a marvelous set of assessment rubric generators, free of charge. If, however, you wish to subscribe to their full service, there is a modest subscription fee.

Another alternative is to use fully modifiable rubric generators available free at **RubiStar**, which is supported by the U.S. Department of Education. To reach RubiStar, type http://rubistar.4teachers.org/index.shtml into your browser's address box.

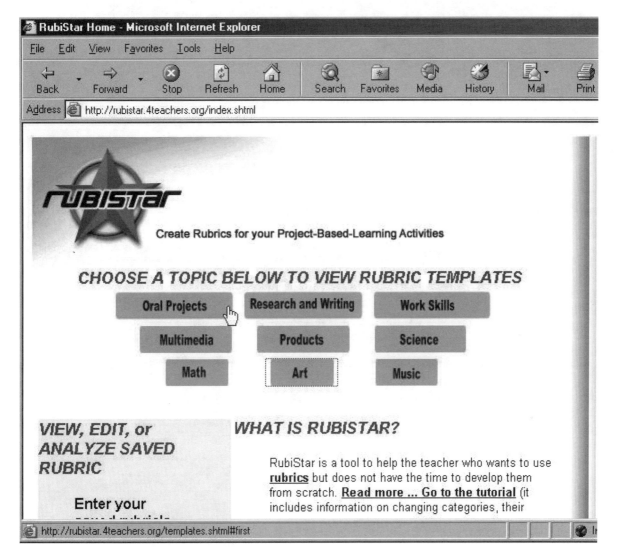

Select **Oral Projects** from the choices above.

You may also choose to create your rubric in Spanish for ESL students.

Select **Multimedia Project** from the list provided.

Read through the directions for creating this rubric and fill in the requested information.

Select **Descriptive** or **Numerical Rating Scale** and continue through the Category selections. Modify the contents of each category's text box by scrolling over and highlighting the text and replacing it with the assessment text you desire.

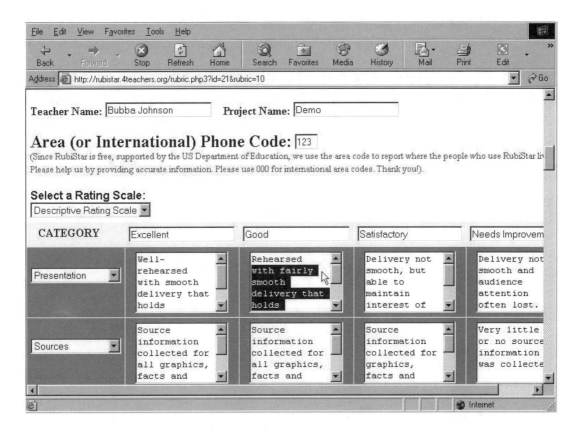

Scroll to the bottom of the screen and click on **Make a Printable Rubric**. You may also choose to **Save** your rubrics on RubiStar's server. By clicking on **Make and Save a Printable Rubric**, your rubrics can be saved for as long as 18 months.

Why save your rubric?

- Edit your rubrics at any time.
- Create custom categories and rows.
- Rubrics will be kept in our system for 18 months.

Section 16 — Summation

What have You Learned from this Book?

It is my sincerest hope that this book was both easy to read and user friendly. I purposefully developed it using plain language to make your transition to technology integration. Remember that technology is just one more vehicle to use for the delivery of curriculum. It is intended to compliment, not drive it.

I attempted to organize each section in a logical, progressive manner, allowing the reader to continually build their knowledge base and skill levels. Hopefully, it's easy to follow step-by-step screen captures aided the process.

You have learned how to locate the Internet's searching tools such as Fossick, Google, Mamma, Vivisimo, and a host of others. You also learned how to create a keyword search for the information you are seeking.

Of special importance, you learned how to create fun, exciting, multimedia-type lesson plans, as well as where to find hundreds of thousands of them already online. You also learned what an Internet-based learning project is all about, and how to locate, join in, or create an exciting learning adventure for your class.

Technology is changing the way we teach, the way students learn, and the way the world thinks. As educators, we must continue to be flexible in our approach to teaching. As Einstein said, "Imagination is more important than knowledge." We owe it to our students and to ourselves to find new ways to motivate and engage them in using new educational technology tools.

The Future of Technology in Our Schools

To quote a phrase from the *Outer Limits*, "What's that up ahead, a signpost, pointing the direction to an unknown future." Picture if you will a world where classrooms as we know them no longer exist. Textbooks have evolved into Internet-based learning stations, complete with interactive learning modules. Students are grouped together heterogeneously in specially equipped, technology laden rooms. The course teacher is sequestered in a remote location, beaming directions for the learning modules via wireless devices that enable them to communicate with the group or an individual student. The teacher can remotely access each student's learning module, send electronic suggestions, and monitor student behavior. Students, in turn, communicate voice and text messages to each other and the teacher via specialized communication tools such as Blackberries, Palm Pilots, and other hand-held devices. The miniaturization of computing devices is governed only by the ability of the naked eye to read the smaller screens.

If the mere possibility of the above scenario sounds unsettling, it should. Considering all of our human failings, it has been and will always be, the direct human interaction between teacher and student that make the real differences in student learning, positive self-esteem, and achievement. Isaac Asimov once said, "Wouldn't it be wonderful if humans were as compassionate, warm, protective, and understanding as we expect robots to be?" The fact is that nothing will ever replace the human contact that only a living, warm, compassionate, and understanding teacher can provide.

Certainly, there are circumstances where the above unsettling scenario can be of value, for instance, in a situation where a child is at home recovering from an illness, or lives in a remote part of the globe where attending a formalized school is unrealistic. Even then, a caring supportive teacher can and will make all the difference.

Fortunately, or unfortunately, the face of technology in the classroom is changing by leaps and bounds, almost faster than technology integration experts can assimilate it. Corporate America is feeding more and more technology innovations into the mix, keeping even the fast-footed among us gasping for a leveling-off point to catch our collective breaths. The next level of technology development seems to appear with each passing month rather than year.

The unfortunate aspect of this scenario is that schools across the globe are ill equipped to deal with the ever-burgeoning growth of technology. Most classroom teachers are lucky to have one computer, let alone three or four. They are being asked to ensure that all students have quality exposure and sufficient time to gain a thorough working knowledge of technology, its uses, and what role it plays in their future. Though most teachers do the best they can, the truth is that they just don't have enough resources, hardware or software, to make it happen.

While Internet and computer use in our classrooms is surely on the upswing, we are going to have to increase funding for hardware, software, and especially professional development. If teachers are not properly trained to use emerging technologies, how can we expect them to teach our students?

Students who are not technology literate will face an uncertain future at the hands of a more demanding Corporate America. It is up to our schools to ensure that students are properly prepared for the future.

The computer age is upon us and will only become more a part of our lives. Children need to be introduced to computers at an early age, to help them keep up with the near-constant changes. Schools must realize that an effective education of our children must include computer programs and the Internet.

CD-ROMs containing interactive software packages provide students with the opportunity to view sample test questions and answers, and even an assessment rubric must be included for each section of the new digital textbooks.

Schools must gradually move away from traditional classroom instructional models and begin to realize that, like speed limits, technology is not merely a suggestion; rather, it is becoming mandatory. Schools must make the most effective use of even the limited technology they possess to help students become the knowledge workers of the 21st century. What does your signpost say?